D1997549

Weekly

Real-World Writing

GRADES 5–6

Writing: Nancy Balter
Content Editing: Kathleen Jorgensen
Copy Editing: Cathy Harber
Art Direction: Yuki Meyer
Illustration: Bryan Langdo
Cover Design: Yuki Meyer
Design/Production: Paula Acojido
Yuki Meyer

EMC 6079

Evan-Moor®

Visit *teaching-standards.com* to view a correlation of this book. This is a free service.

Correlated to Current Standards

Congratulations on your purchase of some of the finest teaching materials in the world.

For information about other Evan-Moor products, call 1-800-777-4362, fax 1-800-777-4332, or visit our website, www.evan-moor.com.

18 Lower Ragsdale Drive, Monterey, CA 93940-5746. Printed in USA.

001

CPSIA: McNaughton & Gunn, Saline, MI USA [2/2022]

CONTENTS

What's in *Weekly Real-World Writing*

Most writing programs cover the essentials of academic writing that students need to succeed in school: grammar and mechanics, structure of sentences and paragraphs, and the essential parts of fiction and nonfiction genres. While some academic writing may play a role in students' everyday lives, we use many other types of writing on a daily basis—on paper, online, and in graphic form. This series covers many of those writing formats.

24 Engaging Units

Real-world writing happens when there is a reason to write. The format of the writing often follows the writing purpose. This book focuses on six common writing purposes: self-expression, information, evaluation, inquiry, analysis, and persuasion. Within each purpose are four units, each featuring a different writing format. The first two units in each purpose section are geared toward grade 5 and the second two are geared toward grade 6, but feel free to use whatever is suitable for your students.

Unit Features

Units are designed to fit into a weekly lesson plan. Each 5-page unit provides a page of information for the teacher, followed by modeling for the students, a graphic organizer, and writing tasks.

Teacher Overview

Describes the writing format and explains its relevance and contexts for use

Features often included in the format (also reflected in the graphic organizer)

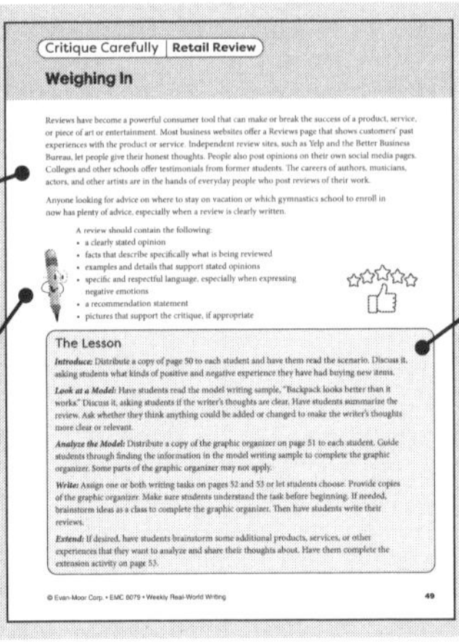

A suggested plan for introducing the writing format and model writing sample, leading student discussions, using the graphic organizer, and assigning writing tasks

Scenario and Model Writing Sample

A scenario in which the writing format might be used

A model writing sample resulting from the scenario; demonstrates the use of the format features

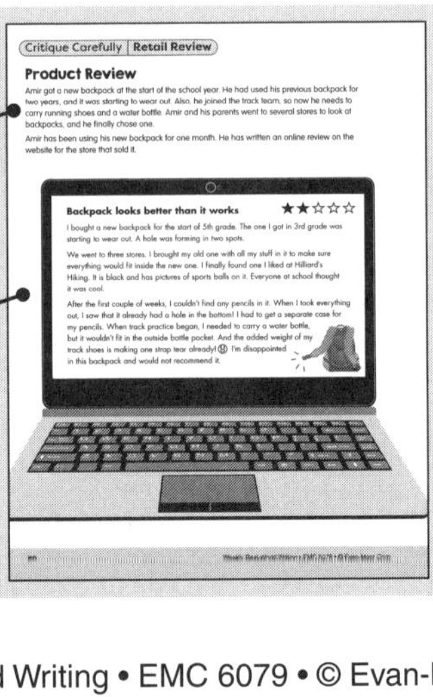

Format-Specific Graphic Organizer

A way to collect notes for the format in the unit; includes sections for most of the format features listed in the Teacher Overview

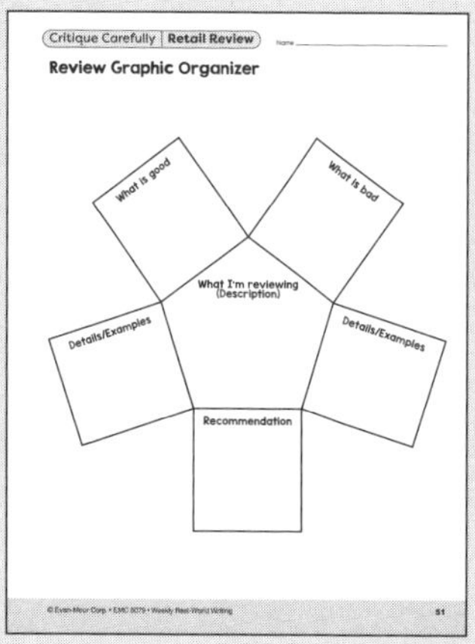

Writing Tasks

Two opportunities to practice writing in the given format, along with response space

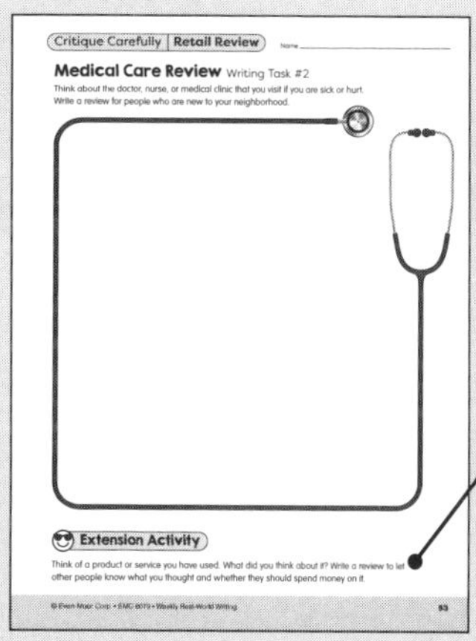

An extension activity that provides an opportunity for students to relate the format to their own lives

Student Rubrics

Two student rubrics are provided, one for formal writing and one for informal writing. These are general, non-format-specific rubrics to remind students of the general aspects of effective writing. (pages 7 and 8)

Have students use the formal writing rubric to check formal formats, such as a business letter or a report. Have them use the informal writing rubric to check informal formats, such as a journal entry or a lost-and-found notice.

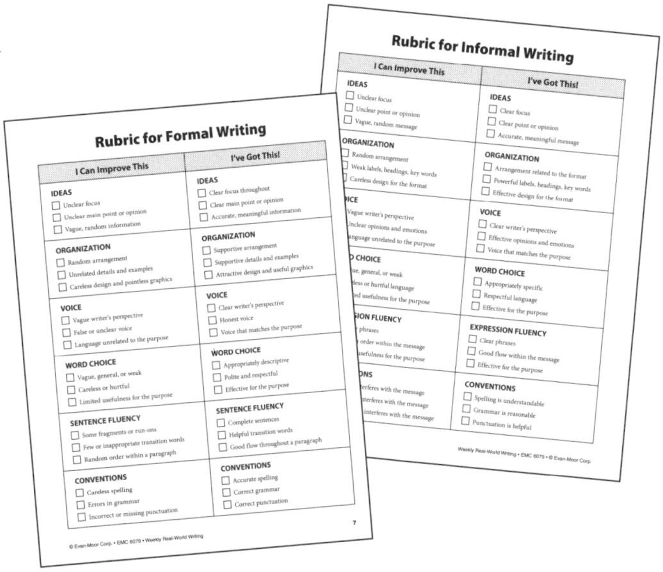

Ways to Use *Weekly Real-World Writing*

Connections for Your Students

You can use the units in this series in many ways. Use the units to extend your primary writing program, providing additional writing opportunities. Use them to augment learning in other content areas. For example, you can use the Blog or Opinion Letter units to have students process their thoughts on current events that you are studying in social studies. You can use the Peer Feedback unit before having students use peer review in science or math. You can use the Thank-you Note unit to thank a guest speaker who has visited your class. Be on the lookout for everyday opportunities to relate units to your students' real lives.

The Importance of Discussion

Discussing the scenario and the model writing sample does more than show students why people write. Just as important as what the writer wants to say is making sure the audience understands what the writer intended. The writer must understand the audience's perspective: Does the audience merely lack knowledge? Are they curious about something? Do they have an attitude or belief that is different from the writer's? Will they most likely be happy, sad, or defensive about the writer's message? By anticipating the audience's perspective, the writer can choose words carefully and organize the writing to avoid an unwanted reaction. Discussing both the writer's and the reader's perspectives in the unit scenario will help students understand how writing, feelings, and relationships are related.

Use of Graphic Organizers

The main purpose of the graphic organizer is to help students get started and plan what they will write. However, it can also be used to analyze the model writing sample. Lead students to connect a sample format's components with the graphic organizer by asking questions such as, "A blog entry has a specific focus. What is the focus in the sample? Write it in the Focus box on your graphic organizer," or "A product review should mention both good and bad things. What was a good thing mentioned in the sample? Write it in the 'What is good' section on your graphic organizer."

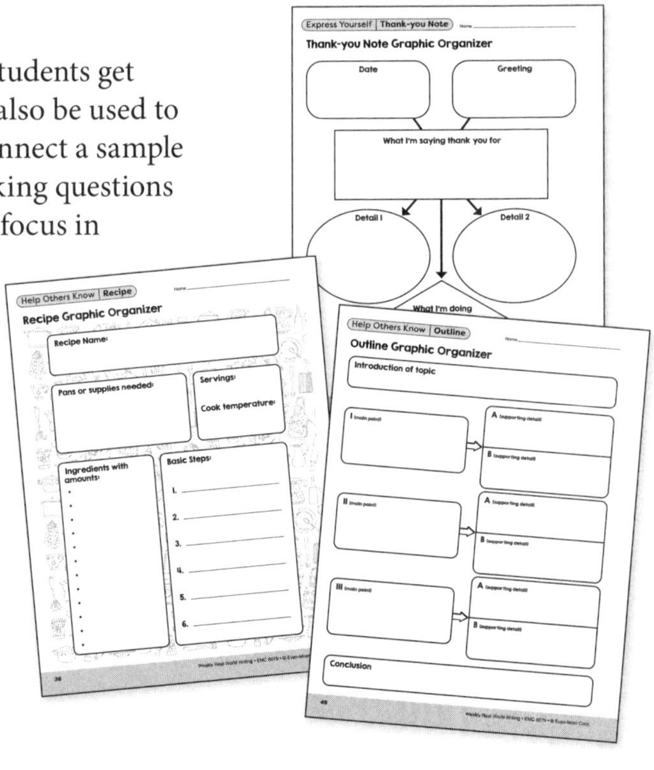

Rubric for Formal Writing

I Can Improve This	I've Got This!
IDEAS ☐ Unclear focus ☐ Unclear main point or opinion ☐ Vague, random information	**IDEAS** ☐ Clear focus throughout ☐ Clear main point or opinion ☐ Accurate, meaningful information
ORGANIZATION ☐ Random arrangement ☐ Unrelated details and examples ☐ Careless design and pointless graphics	**ORGANIZATION** ☐ Supportive arrangement ☐ Supportive details and examples ☐ Attractive design and useful graphics
VOICE ☐ Vague writer's perspective ☐ False or unclear voice ☐ Language unrelated to the purpose	**VOICE** ☐ Clear writer's perspective ☐ Honest voice ☐ Voice that matches the purpose
WORD CHOICE ☐ Vague, general, or weak ☐ Careless or hurtful ☐ Limited usefulness for the purpose	**WORD CHOICE** ☐ Appropriately descriptive ☐ Polite and respectful ☐ Effective for the purpose
SENTENCE FLUENCY ☐ Some fragments or run-ons ☐ Few or inappropriate transition words ☐ Random order within a paragraph	**SENTENCE FLUENCY** ☐ Complete sentences ☐ Helpful transition words ☐ Good flow throughout a paragraph
CONVENTIONS ☐ Careless spelling ☐ Errors in grammar ☐ Incorrect or missing punctuation	**CONVENTIONS** ☐ Accurate spelling ☐ Correct grammar ☐ Correct punctuation

Rubric for Informal Writing

I Can Improve This	I've Got This!
IDEAS ☐ Unclear focus ☐ Unclear point or opinion ☐ Vague, random message	**IDEAS** ☐ Clear focus ☐ Clear point or opinion ☐ Accurate, meaningful message
ORGANIZATION ☐ Random arrangement ☐ Weak labels, headings, key words ☐ Careless design for the format	**ORGANIZATION** ☐ Arrangement related to the format ☐ Powerful labels, headings, key words ☐ Effective design for the format
VOICE ☐ Vague writer's perspective ☐ Unclear opinions and emotions ☐ Language unrelated to the purpose	**VOICE** ☐ Clear writer's perspective ☐ Effective opinions and emotions ☐ Voice that matches the purpose
WORD CHOICE ☐ Vague, general, or weak ☐ Careless or hurtful language ☐ Limited usefulness for the purpose	**WORD CHOICE** ☐ Appropriately specific ☐ Respectful language ☐ Effective for the purpose
EXPRESSION FLUENCY ☐ Unclear phrases ☐ Random order within the message ☐ Limited usefulness for the purpose	**EXPRESSION FLUENCY** ☐ Clear phrases ☐ Good flow within the message ☐ Effective for the purpose
CONVENTIONS ☐ Spelling interferes with the message ☐ Grammar interferes with the message ☐ Punctuation interferes with the message	**CONVENTIONS** ☐ Spelling is understandable ☐ Grammar is reasonable ☐ Punctuation is helpful

Keeping a Journal

Some people think keeping a diary is something only children do. In reality, many adults keep diaries or journals. Some even feel that doing so helps them be more successful. There are benefits to keeping a diary. It helps the writer remember events, feelings, or thoughts that might be forgotten. Many people who write lists or plans in their journals often feel more organized. Writing down thoughts on paper can help release feelings that have been held back, allowing the writer to get a better perspective on a situation. Some people keep gratitude journals to focus on the good things in their lives. Daily, consistent writing also improves overall writing skills.

A journal or diary can be kept anywhere—online, on a computer, or in a notebook, a lockable diary, or a sketchbook. Just keep it together in one place.

A journal or diary entry should contain the following:

- the date
- your own voice and truthful thoughts or opinions
- descriptive language explaining who, what, where, when, why, and how
- drawings or photos if they are useful
- the right amount of space needed to tell each story

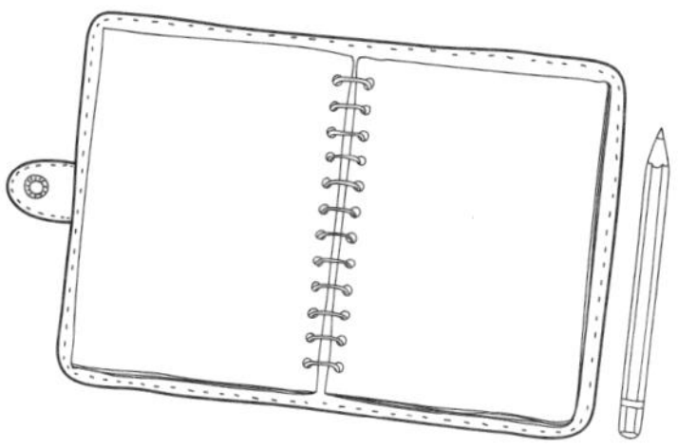

The Lesson

Introduce: Using the information above, explain to students what a journal is. Then distribute a copy of page 10 to each student and have them read the scenario. Discuss it, asking students if they've ever kept a diary or journal and why.

Look at a Model: Have students read the model writing sample, "The Argument." Discuss it, asking students what they can figure out about what Sophie feels, thinks, or wants to express. Ask whether they think anything could be added or changed to help Sophie better remember the events or express her thoughts and feelings.

Analyze the Model: Distribute a copy of the graphic organizer on page 11 to each student. Guide students through finding the information in the model writing sample to complete the graphic organizer. Some parts of the graphic organizer may not apply.

Write: Assign and provide copies of one or both writing tasks on pages 12 and 13 or let students choose. Also provide copies of the graphic organizer. Make sure students understand the task before beginning. If needed, brainstorm ideas as a class to complete the graphic organizer. Then have students write their journal entries.

Extend: If desired, have students brainstorm some journal topics that inspire them. Have them complete the extension activity on page 13 on a separate sheet of paper.

My Life in Black and White

Sophie started keeping a diary because she wants to be a writer one day. She thought daily writing would help her become a better writer. She also wants to be able to better remember events in her life and her feelings about them.

Sophie has been keeping a diary for about two years. In this entry, she writes about an argument she had with a friend.

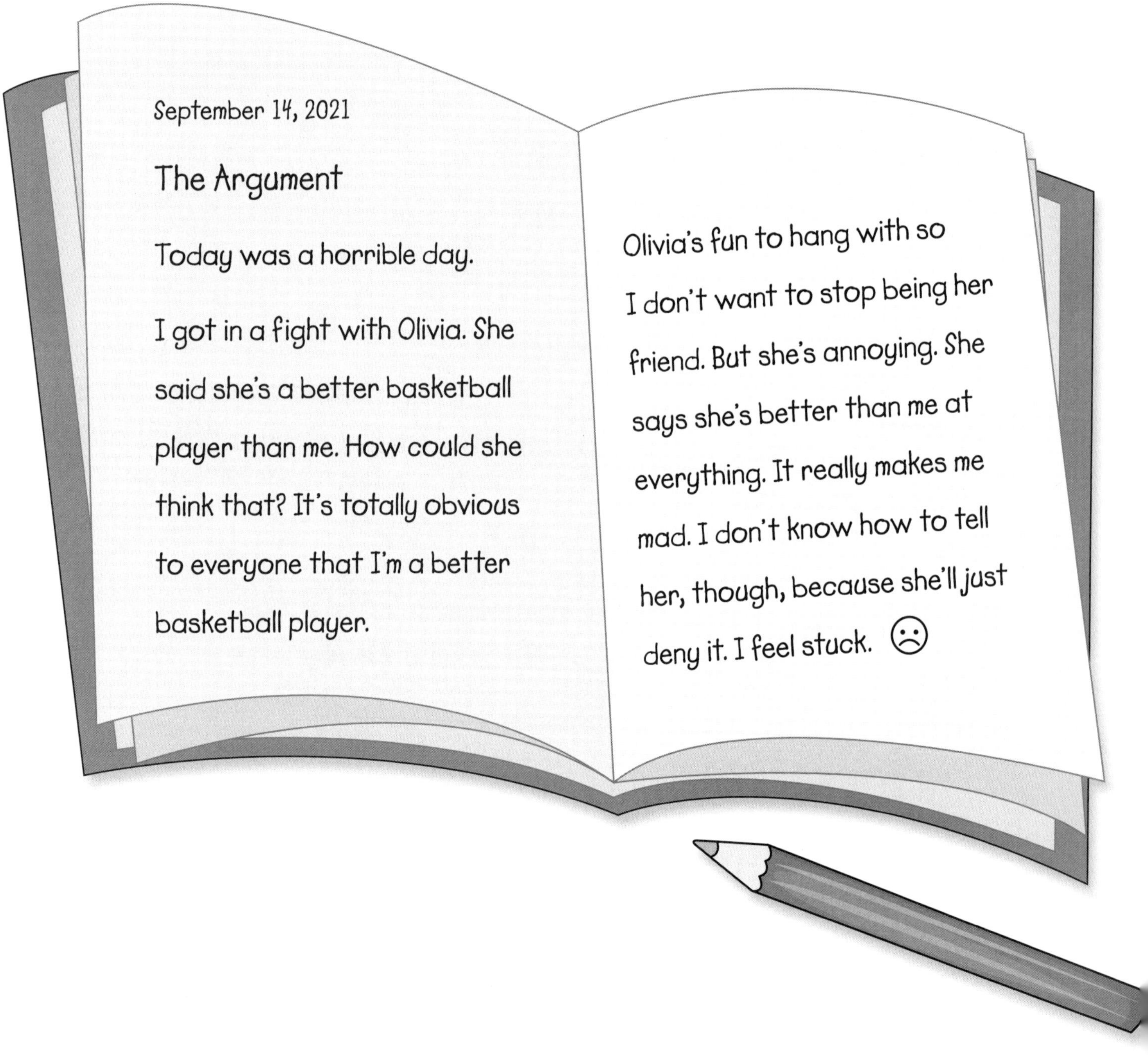

Name ____________________

Journal Entry Graphic Organizer

Who?

Where?

When?

What happened? Why?

How do you feel about it?

Outcome that you would like:

Name ____________________

My Stressed-out Life! Writing Task #1

Imagine that it is October and you are feeling very stressed about all your work at school. You have lots of homework and a math test coming up. You are also very busy with the after-school robotics club. Write a journal entry in which you describe your stress. List what you need to do. Brainstorm some ways to get your work done and feel calmer.

Name ____________________

Keep Those Thoughts Coming Writing Task #2

Becoming a better writer often involves simply writing more. Set a timer for 5 minutes. Challenge yourself to write for the entire time without stopping. If you get stuck, write down anything that comes to mind. It's fine to keep switching topics. Use the back of the paper if needed. Don't worry about fixing grammar or spelling. Just write!

Extension Activity

Try keeping a journal or diary every day for a week. At the end of the week, reread what you wrote. Reflect on whether writing every day helped you in any way.

Expressing Thanks

Saying "thank you" is an important part of our relationship with others. People love to know that their gift was appreciated. A thank-you note also confirms that a mailed gift arrived. There is even an advantage to the writer—taking time to express gratitude and think about the good things in our lives improves our overall mental health.

Thank-you notes can be sent in the mail or hand-delivered. They can also be sent in an e-mail or on social media. They are usually written, but you can send a recorded audio or video note, too.

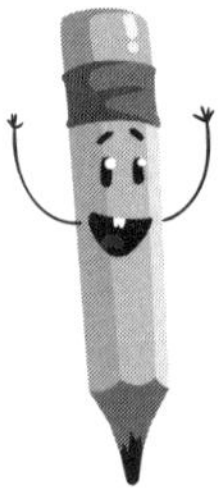

A thank-you note should contain the following:

- the date
- a greeting
- what you are thanking the note's recipient for
- details about why you liked the gift or how you'll use it
- a comment about what you are doing now or in the near future
- your name or signature

The Lesson

Introduce: Using the information above, explain to students what a thank-you note is. Then distribute a copy of page 15 to each student and have them read the scenario. Discuss it, asking students how they feel when they receive gifts or when someone does something nice for them. Also ask how they feel about giving gifts or doing nice things for others. Ask if and how others express thanks to them and how that makes them feel.

Look at a Model: Have students read the model writing sample, "Dear Abuelito." Discuss it, asking students what they can figure out about what Rafael received and whether he appropriately expressed gratitude for the gift. Ask whether they think anything could be added or changed to improve the thank-you note.

Analyze the Model: Distribute a copy of the graphic organizer on page 16 to each student. Guide students through finding the information in the model writing sample to complete the graphic organizer. Some parts of the graphic organizer may not apply.

Write: Assign and provide copies of one or both writing tasks on pages 17 and 18 or let students choose. Also provide copies of the graphic organizer. Make sure students understand the task before beginning. If needed, brainstorm ideas as a class to complete the graphic organizer. Then have students write their thank-you notes.

Extend: If desired, have students brainstorm some reasons to write a thank-you note. Have them complete the extension activity on page 18 on a separate sheet of paper.

Birthday Thank-you

Rafael's grandfather took Rafael to lunch and to see a movie for his birthday. Rafael sent a thank-you card to his grandfather. Rafael calls his grandfather "Abuelito."

October 20, 2021

Dear Abuelito,

Thank you so much for my birthday trip! I really enjoyed eating pizza with you. I'm glad you like pineapple on your pizza—just like me. The movie was great!

I hope we can hang out again soon. Maybe I can go to lunch and a movie with you for YOUR birthday!

Thank you for making my birthday so special.

Love,

Rafael

Name ____________________

Thank-you Note Graphic Organizer

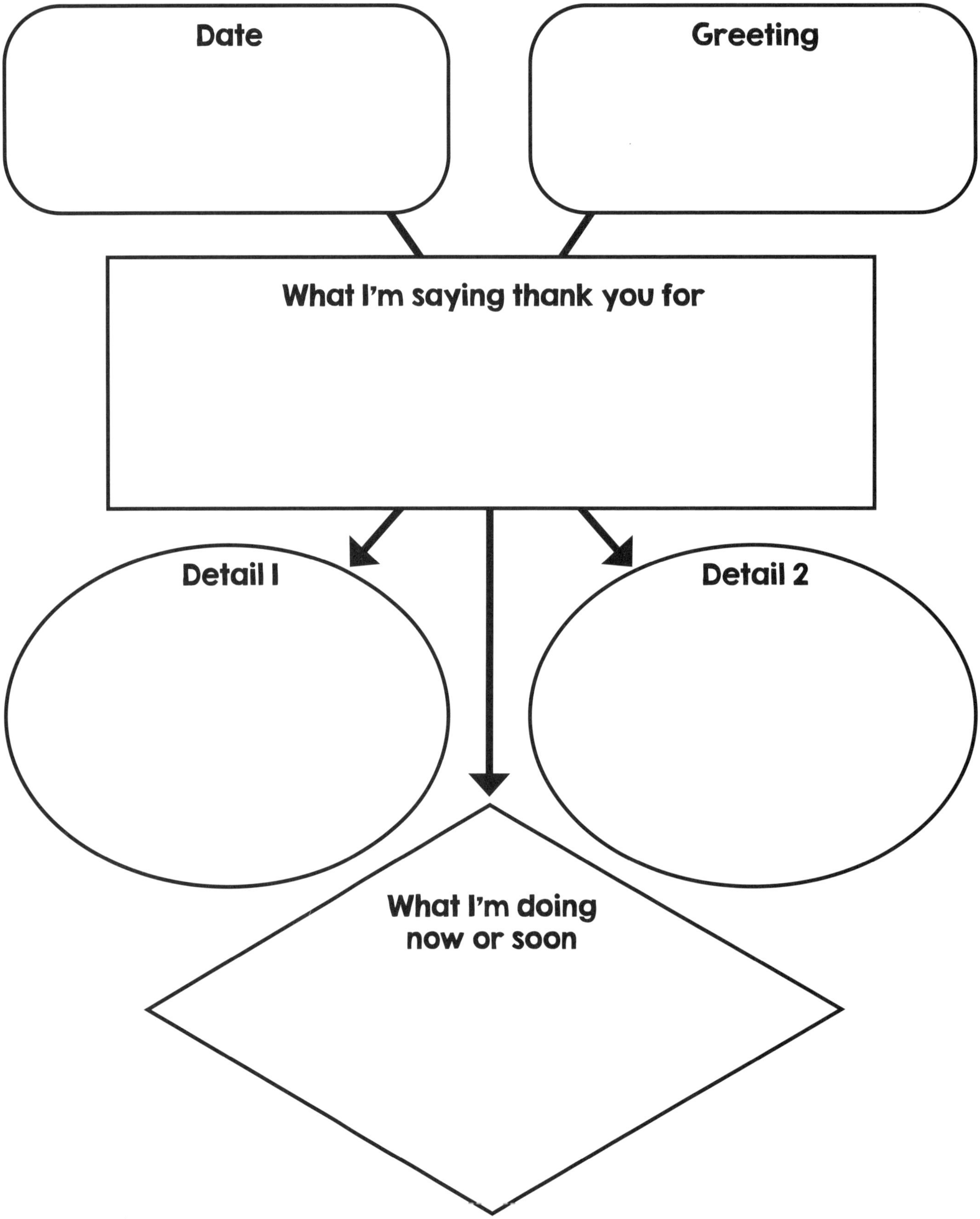

Name ____________________

Souvenir Writing Task #1

Imagine that your friend Pablo brought you a souvenir from a vacation he just took. He gave you a jigsaw puzzle with a picture of your favorite animal on it. Write a thank-you note to Pablo.

Name ____________________

Donation Writing Task #2

Imagine that you participated in a school fundraising jogathon. Donors agreed to pay you a certain amount of money for every mile you jogged. Your aunt donated to your school fundraiser. Write her an e-mail to thank her for donating to your school and to let her know how the event went.

To ____________________

Subject ____________________

Extension Activity

Write and send a thank-you note. It can be for a gift or for doing something thoughtful, such as sharing something with you, helping you, or making you feel better. It will make someone's day!

Sharing Information, Interests, and Insights

Blogging is an effective way to let everyone know what is on your mind. People blog for many reasons. Some want to share a particular journey, such as recovering from a sports injury, getting ready to go off to college, or planning their wedding. Some want to help others by sharing their knowledge or experience. Some want to draw attention to a particular cause, such as the environment or homelessness, or to an interest, such as fitness or music. Businesses and nonprofit organizations use blogs to draw people to their websites.

Writing blog entries offers many benefits to students, but setting up a blog site (or a vlog site, featuring a video blog) must be done carefully to ensure the safety and privacy of students on a public-facing site. Students must have permission and involvement from parents to launch a blog or vlog online.

A blog entry should contain the following:

- a specific focus
- a logical organization
- the writer's authentic voice
- correct grammar, spelling, and punctuation
- graphics that support the text

The Lesson

Introduce: Using the information above, explain to students what a blog is. Then distribute a copy of page 20 to each student and have them read the scenario. Discuss it, asking students why they think Dimitry started a blog instead of a journal. Why would others read it? Ask what kinds of blogs they read and why.

Look at a Model: Have students read the model writing sample, "18 Days to Go." Discuss it, asking students what they can figure out about what Dimitry feels, thinks, and is learning. Ask whether they think anything could be added or changed to know more about what Dimitry is going through.

Analyze the Model: Distribute a copy of the graphic organizer on page 21 to each student. Guide students through finding the information in the model writing sample to complete the graphic organizer. Some parts of the graphic organizer may not apply.

Write: Assign and provide copies of one or both writing tasks on pages 22 and 23 or let students choose. Also provide copies of the graphic organizer. Make sure students understand the task before beginning. If needed, brainstorm ideas as a class to complete the graphic organizer. Then have students write their blog entries.

Extend: If desired, have students brainstorm some blog topics that inspire them. Have them complete the extension activity on page 23 on a separate sheet of paper.

The Big Move

Dimitry and his family are moving across Canada, from Alberta to Ontario. He has never lived anywhere else. He is both nervous and excited. He is also very busy, helping his family pack their belongings and saying goodbye to his friends.

Dimitry started a blog the day after his mother announced that they were moving at the end of the school year. In this entry, he writes about his progress and also responds to some of his readers' comments.

18 Days to Go

Today I finished sorting what I am taking and what I am giving away. I feel like I'm giving up my childhood. But I know that someone else will enjoy my old games, and the apartment we're moving into won't be so cluttered. I think I will miss my view of the prairie—quiet space, my neighbors' horses, the occasional moose off the highway—even more than my things.

Thanks to the readers who have posted their stories about moving. It seems like everyone adjusts eventually. You just have to accept your new place and be open to change and to making new friends. And you don't really leave your old friends behind as long as you take them with you on your journey.

Name ______________________

Blog Graphic Organizer

Focus

Details

Organization

Proofread:

- ☐ grammar
- ☐ spelling
- ☐ punctuation

Graphics

Name ____________________________

Food and Fitness Blog Writing Task #1

Melissa loves food and fitness. She enjoys exploring different ethnic foods and foods that give her lots of energy. She also likes activities that keep her heart and muscles strong. Imagine that you are Melissa. Write a blog entry about one of the things she loves.

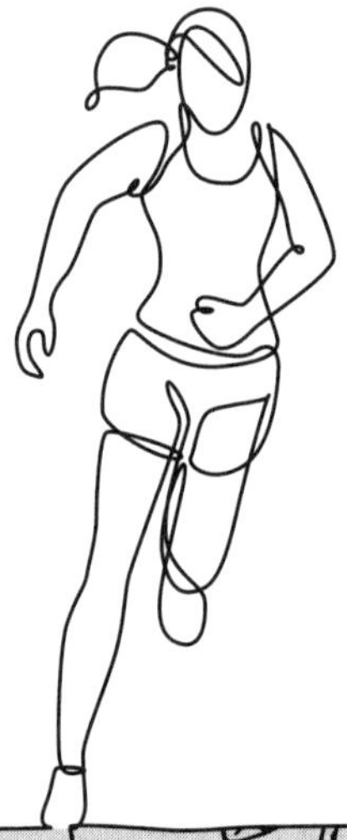

Name ____________________

Public Transportation Blog Writing Task #2

Imagine that you work for the company that provides public transportation in your city. This company has buses, electric light-rail, and commuter trains, along with rental bikes and scooters. Write an entry for the company's blog about the benefits to the environment, the cost savings, or the convenience of using public transportation.

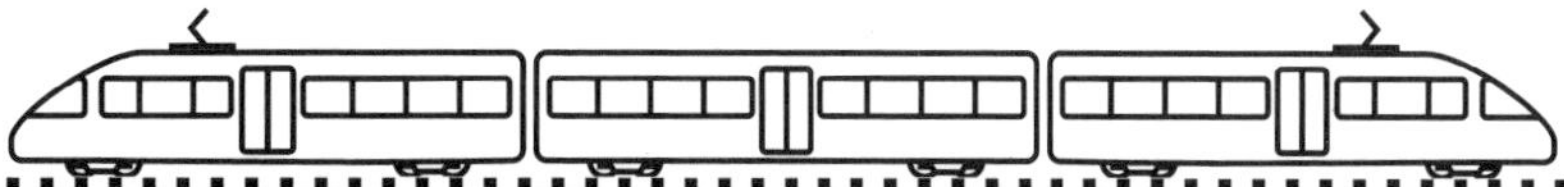

Extension Activity

Choose a topic or an experience that you would like others to know about. Think about the type of people who would want to read it. Write a blog entry for those people to read and respond to.

My Name in Print

Opinion letters are often letters to the editor of a newspaper. They provide a way for the public to respond to a published article. Sometimes a letter to the editor offers additional support for the viewpoint in the original article. Other times, someone may disagree and want to provide another opinion. Letters are widely read by the public—including lawmakers—and can affect others' thinking. It can be exciting to have your ideas published.

Opinion letters are often sent to the newspaper by e-mail or traditional mail. They may also be posted on social media as an open letter. A clearly written opinion letter is valuable to readers, whether they are looking for a different perspective, a supporting perspective, or just a clearer understanding of an issue.

An opinion letter should contain the following:

- a clearly stated opinion in response to a recent topic
- supporting ideas and examples for your point of view or solution to a problem
- an explanation of how the topic relates to your local community
- specific and respectful language, especially when expressing negative emotions
- your name; indicate if you have special knowledge about the topic
- correct grammar, spelling, and punctuation

The Lesson

Introduce: Using the information above, explain to students what an opinion letter is. Then distribute a copy of page 25 to each student and have them read the scenario. Discuss it, asking students if they've ever read or heard an opinion about a news event that they strongly agreed or disagreed with and why.

Look at a Model: Have students read the model writing sample, "Our Lunch, Our Choice." Discuss it, asking students if the writer's thoughts are clear. Have students summarize the letter. Ask whether they think anything could be added or changed to make the writer's thoughts more clear or relevant.

Analyze the Model: Distribute a copy of the graphic organizer on page 26 to each student. Guide students through finding the information in the model writing sample to complete the graphic organizer. Some parts of the graphic organizer may not apply.

Write: Assign and provide copies of one or both writing tasks on pages 27 and 28 or let students choose. Also provide copies of the graphic organizer. Make sure students understand the task before beginning. If needed, brainstorm ideas as a class to complete the graphic organizer. Give students time to research the topics. Then have students write their opinion letters.

Extend: If desired, have students brainstorm topics they have strong opinions about, or bring in copies of editorials or local news articles. Have them complete the extension activity on page 28 on a separate sheet of paper.

Darnell Writes Back

There was an editorial in the local paper about school lunches. The author said that the menu needed to be revised. In particular, pizza should not be offered daily. Too many kids were choosing pizza every single day and not getting well-rounded nutrition. The menu should rotate pizza with other foods such as fish, chicken, and tofu so that students can try new foods and be healthier.

Darnell strongly disagrees with cutting pizza from the daily school lunch menu. He responded by e-mailing a letter to the editor of the newspaper.

Our Lunch, Our Choice

To: editor@baysidebeacon.com

Subject: School lunch menu

To the Editor:

On November 20, your newspaper wrote that pizza should be cut from the daily school lunch menu. I strongly disagree. Many kids like pizza and do not like the other meals you suggested. If those foods are served instead of pizza, lots of kids will skip lunch and go hungry during their afternoon classes. Being hungry is not good for concentration in school. It's possible to give kids well-rounded nutrition by offering different pizza toppings—both meats and vegetables. Plus, you did not think about vegetarians, like me. We will not eat the meat and fish you suggested. Veggie pizza is always a good choice for vegetarians. The school lunch menu should be changed only after talking to students and understanding what we need. Please do not suggest getting rid of pizza as a daily option.

Sincerely,

Darnell Williams

Name ____________________

Opinion Letter Graphic Organizer

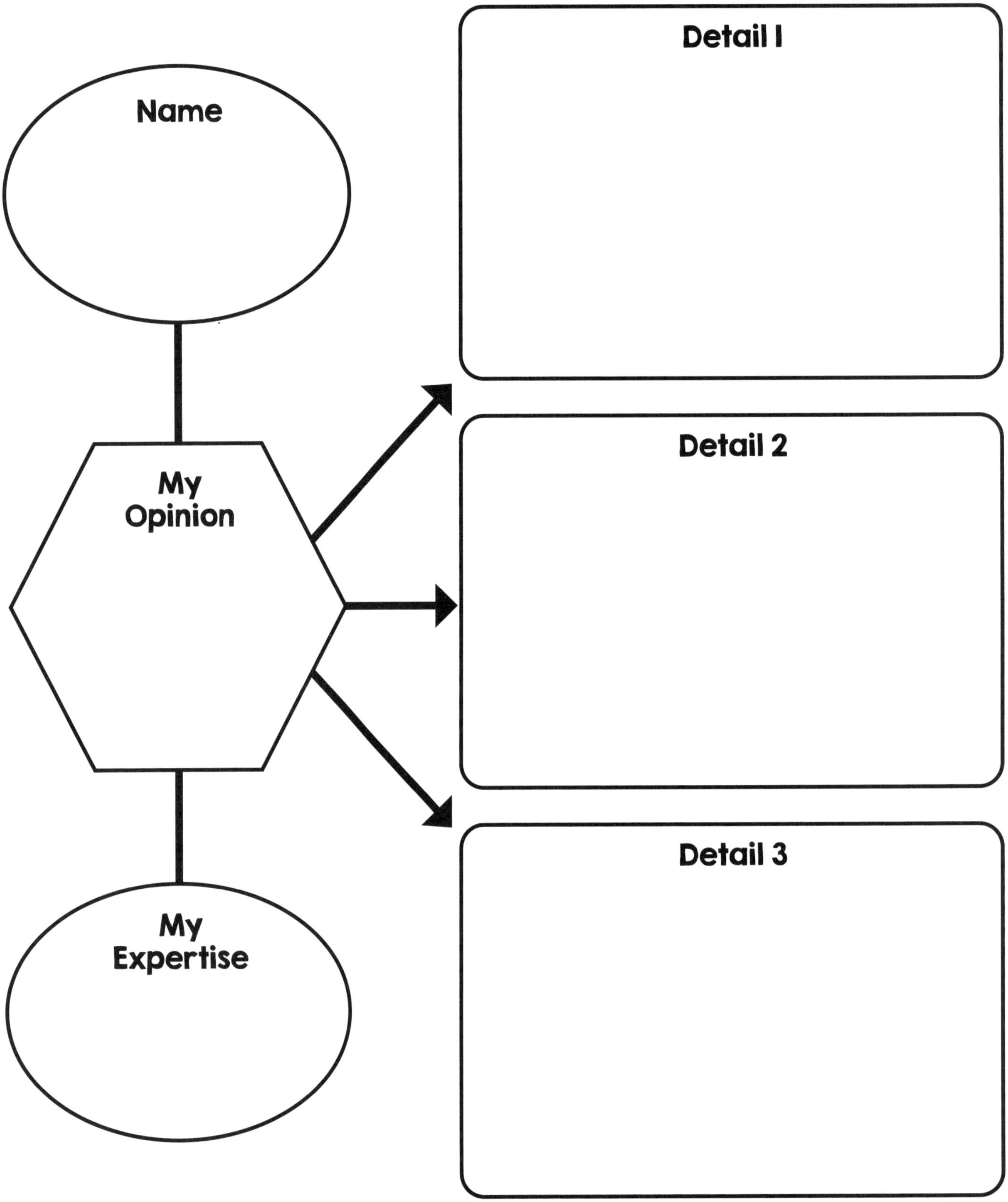

Name ______________________________

Youth Center Letter Writing Task #1

Imagine that someone has written to the local paper to suggest closing the youth center to save taxpayer money. Many people think that youth and after-school centers are necessary. Research reasons why towns have them and how much they cost to run. Write a letter to the editor stating whether keeping the youth center open is important and explaining your opinion.

Name ____________________

School Uniforms Letter Writing Task #2

Imagine that the new head of your school district was interviewed on the local TV news. She said that students in the district should wear uniforms to school so all students will feel like they belong. Do you agree or disagree with this statement? Write an opinion letter to the TV station to support or object to school uniforms.

Extension Activity

Look through your local paper (online or in print). Choose an issue that is important to you. Write a letter to the editor explaining your opinion on the issue. Send a copy of your letter to the paper and see if it is published.

Can You Help Me Find My...?

We all lose things and know that terrible feeling when something valuable goes missing. That's why we feel sympathy when we find something valuable, such as a lost pet, a purse, or even a well-loved child's toy. There's always a moment of panic about what to do about the situation. Fortunately, many neighbors are willing to help find and return things. Posting lost-or-found notices around town, in neighborhood apps, and even in the local paper can be the key to getting beloved pets and other items back to their owners. It's important that the notice contain certain information to make the process quicker and more likely to be successful.

A lost-or-found notice should contain the following:

- a clear description of what you are looking for or what you found
- a picture of the item or pet, if possible
- the date the item or pet went missing or was found
- where the item or pet was last seen or where it is located now
- contact information
- offer of a reward, if appropriate

The Lesson

Introduce: Using the information above, explain to students what a lost-and-found notice is. Then distribute a copy of page 30 to each student and have them read the scenario. Discuss it, asking students how people who saw Rohan's poster probably felt. Ask students if they have ever lost or found something valuable. Ask them how they felt or would feel.

Look at a Model: Have students read the model writing sample, "Lost: DOG!" Discuss it, asking students if they understand what was missing and how to return it. Ask students how much the picture helps. Ask whether they think anything could be added or changed in the notice.

Analyze the Model: Distribute a copy of the graphic organizer on page 31 to each student. Guide students through finding the information in the model writing sample to complete the graphic organizer. Some parts of the graphic organizer may not apply.

Write: Assign and provide copies of one or both writing tasks on pages 32 and 33 or let students choose. Also provide copies of the graphic organizer. Make sure students understand the task before beginning. If needed, brainstorm ideas as a class to complete the graphic organizer. Then have students write their lost-or-found notices.

Extend: If desired, have students brainstorm some additional situations in their own lives in which writing a lost-or-found notice would be useful. Have them complete the extension activity on page 33 on a separate sheet of paper.

Calling Ollie!

Rohan was walking his dog, Ollie, in the park when Ollie somehow slipped off his leash. Ollie ran after another dog and disappeared. Rohan was very worried about his buddy and made the following poster to ask neighbors for help finding his dog.

Lost: DOG!

Please help me find my dog. His name is Ollie. He got lost in Leafy Park on July 31.

- Poodle with tan-colored curly hair
- Weighs 10 pounds
- Wears an orange collar with his name and our phone number on it

If you have <u>any</u> information about Ollie, please call us at

(123) 456-7890.

Name ______________________

Lost-and-Found Notice Graphic Organizer

What was lost or found?

Description

Picture

Date missing or found

Where last seen or found

Contact information

Reward

 Name ________________

Look What I Found Writing Task #1

Imagine that you found a pair of sunglasses outside a restaurant named Pancake Palace. You turned in the sunglasses to the restaurant manager. Pancake Palace is located at 321 Main Street, and their phone number is 555-1000. You work with your parents to create a neighborhood social media post to let the community know what you found and how to get the sunglasses back. Write your social media post here.

Name ____________________

Help Get Me Home! Writing Task #2

Imagine that your pet cat escaped. Make a poster about your lost cat. Don't use your real contact information for this assignment; make up a phone number or an e-mail address.

Extension Activity

Think back to a time that you found something valuable. Write a found notice for the item. Make up a contact phone number or an e-mail address instead of using your real one.

May I Please Have the Recipe?

Many people love to experiment in the kitchen. If cooks ever want to re-create a tasty tidbit that they just created, they need to write down how they made it. And sooner or later, others are going to ask for the recipe. They might even want to submit it to a recipe competition!

Recipes have a standard format, which makes it easier for everyone to follow. All the ingredients are listed in one section. The preparation and cooking or baking directions are listed in another. Some cooks handwrite their recipes on preprinted recipe cards. Others type them or keep them online.

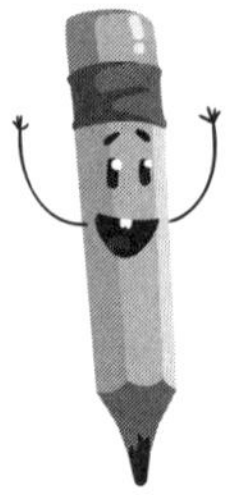

A recipe should contain the following:

- a descriptive and mouthwatering name
- the number of servings it makes
- the list of ingredients and the amounts needed, listed in order of use
- step-by-step preparation directions
- oven temperature or stovetop heat level and cooking time
- any necessary pans or other cooking supplies
- a photo of the ready-to-eat food item

The Lesson

Introduce: Using the information above, explain to students what a recipe is. Then distribute a copy of page 35 to each student and have them read the scenario. Discuss it, asking students if they have ever followed—or even made up—a recipe.

Look at a Model: Have students read the model writing sample, "Oatmeal Pancakes." Discuss it, asking students if they could understand how to make the pancakes. Ask whether they think anything could be added or changed to make the recipe more clear.

Analyze the Model: Distribute a copy of the graphic organizer on page 36 to each student. Guide students through finding the information in the model writing sample to complete the graphic organizer. Some parts of the graphic organizer may not apply.

Write: Assign and provide copies of one or both writing tasks on pages 37 and 38 or let students choose. Also provide copies of the graphic organizer. Make sure students understand the task before beginning. If needed, brainstorm ideas as a class to complete the graphic organizer. Then have students write their recipes.

Extend: If desired, have students brainstorm situations in their own lives in which they might want to write down a recipe. Have them complete the extension activity on page 38 on a separate sheet of paper.

How to Make Pancakes

Hoda wants to surprise her family by making breakfast this morning. She used a recipe that she made at camp last summer. Here is the recipe that she wrote.

Oatmeal Pancakes

Ingredients

- 2 cups oatmeal
- 1 tablespoon baking powder
- 2 eggs
- 1 cup yogurt
- 2 tablespoons milk
- 2 tablespoons oil

Steps

1. Put all ingredients in a large bowl. Mix well with a fork.
2. Heat up the griddle or frying pan on medium-low heat.
3. Pour $\frac{1}{2}$ cup of pancake batter onto the griddle for each pancake.
4. When the batter bubbles on top, use a spatula to turn the pancakes over.
5. After a minute or two, use the spatula to lift up one pancake. If it is light brown, it is done. Put the pancakes on a plate and pour some more batter onto the griddle or into the pan.
6. Serve quickly with butter, syrup, and fresh fruit!

Makes 12 pancakes

Name ______________________________

Recipe Graphic Organizer

Recipe name:

Pans or supplies needed:

Servings:

Cook temperature:

Ingredients with amounts:

-
-
-
-
-
-
-
-
-
-
-
-

Basic steps:

1. ______________________________
2. ______________________________
3. ______________________________
4. ______________________________
5. ______________________________
6. ______________________________

Name ____________________

How to Make a Pizza Writing Task #1

Imagine that you have a pen pal in another country who has never had pizza. You want your pen pal to try some. Write a recipe for your favorite type of pizza so he or she can make it. Your pen pal can buy a pre-made pizza crust and pizza sauce. Include any cheese and toppings you like. Also include what to bake the pizza on, such as a metal pan.

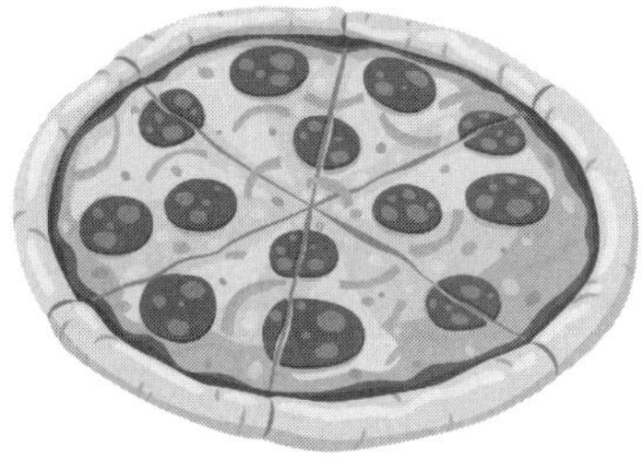

Recipe ____________________

Servings: ____________ **Temperature:** ____________

Ingredients:

Directions:

Name ____________________

Video Recipe Writing Task #2

Watch a cooking or baking video online. Write down the recipe. Pause, rewind, or watch it again as needed so that you catch everything. If the video website provides the written recipe, compare it with your completed recipe.

RECIPE

SERVINGS	TEMPERATURE	DATE

INGREDIENTS	DIRECTIONS

Extension Activity

Write a recipe for a banana split, an ice cream sundae, or another favorite dessert. Ask a family member to follow your recipe—without asking you any questions—and see if it turns out exactly as you expected. If not, think about what you could revise to make your recipe more clear.

All Business

There are a lot of informal ways to communicate in the workplace these days—talking, e-mailing, texting, chat messages, even messages scribbled on sticky notes. Business letters, on the other hand, remain an important formal way to communicate.

People write business letters for different reasons. They may be requesting information, complaining about a problem, or giving information or advice. Business letters are not just for businesses; they can also be written to any other group or organization.

A business letter should contain the following:

- your address
- the date the letter was written
- the name and address of the person you are writing to
- a salutation followed by a colon, such as *Dear Dr. Hassan:*
- short paragraphs explaining your points and what you want to happen
- formal and polite language expressing both facts and feelings
- a closing with a comma, such as *Sincerely,* followed by your handwritten signature and typed name underneath
- correct grammar, spelling, and punctuation

The Lesson

Introduce: Using the information above, explain to students what a business letter is. Then distribute a copy of page 40 to each student and have them read the scenario. Discuss it, asking students what the video company probably thought when they received Sridevi's letter. Ask students why and when people, including students, might need to write a business letter.

Look at a Model: Have students read the model writing sample, "Letter to a Video Game Company." Discuss it, asking students if they understand the reasons this student wrote the letter and what action she was requesting from the company. Ask whether they think anything could be added or changed to improve the letter.

Analyze the Model: Distribute a copy of the graphic organizer on page 41 to each student. Guide students through finding the information in the model writing sample to complete the graphic organizer. Some parts of the graphic organizer may not apply.

Write: Assign and provide copies of one or both writing tasks on pages 42 and 43 or let students choose. Also provide copies of the graphic organizer. Make sure students understand the task before beginning. If needed, brainstorm ideas as a class to complete the graphic organizer. Then have students write their business letters.

Extend: If desired, have students brainstorm issues that are important to them. Have them complete the extension activity on page 43 on a separate sheet of paper.

Please Let Me Advance!

Sridevi loves to play an online video game named HipHop–DanceALot. Players can advance to higher levels by earning points or paying money. She likes to play, earn points, and advance. However, Sridevi can't play very often, so she uses her allowance money to advance and keep up with her friends. Recently the company removed the option of paying money to advance levels. Sridevi wrote a letter to the company to ask them to continue offering that option.

Letter to a Video Game Company

123 Main Street
Pointe, IL 61765

November 3, 2021

HipHop–DanceALot Company
5678 Music Drive
Sunny, FL 33100

To Whom It May Concern:

I love your game! I play it a lot with my friends. My friends play every day, so they often go up about five levels each week! I get to play only on Saturday afternoons, so I can't advance that fast.

I used to pay some of my allowance money to keep up with my friends. But now you don't allow players to pay money to advance levels anymore. I'm writing to complain about that and to ask you to put that option back. My dad won't let me play more often, and it's no fun to play with my friends when I'm way behind them.

Please think about changing this. Thank you for your time.

Sincerely,

Sridevi Adiraju

Sridevi Adiraju

 Name ____________________

Business Letter Graphic Organizer

Sender's address:

Today's date:

Name and address of recipient:

Greeting:

Main points of letter:

Closing:

 Name ________________________

I Have a Complaint Writing Task #1

Imagine that you ordered a toy online from the ZonkBot company. When it arrived, something was wrong with it. Write a letter to the company and explain the problem. Then tell them what you want them to do. You might ask for your money back, have them send you a new one, or ask them to change the way they make this toy.

Name ____________________

At Your Service Writing Task #2

Imagine that you would like to start babysitting to earn some money. You want to let your neighbors know when you're available to babysit, how much you charge, and why you'd be a good babysitter. Maybe you tutor neighborhood students or you have taken a childcare class. Write your neighbors a letter to tell them about your babysitting business.

Extension Activity

Find the name of a local elected official, such as your mayor, congressperson, or other representative. Think about a cause that is important to you, such as saving endangered species, having clean water and air, or improving schools. Write a business letter to that official and let him or her know that you care about this issue. Ask the official to let you know what he or she can do to help.

Outline and Refine

Writing a long paper can be overwhelming. Sometimes a student starts typing a whole bunch of ideas. While that can be a great way to start, it can lead to a jumbled, confused paper at the end. Writing an outline helps organize thoughts, which strengthens the writing. It gives the paper a structure. Further, writing an outline can generate new ideas along the way.

There are many outline formats. Students can use an outline that fits the purpose of the paper they are writing (research, expository, persuasive, essay, etc.). The chosen outline format can vary in length and detail as needed. Students can choose the type of outline they like best. They will practice with a traditional outline in this unit.

An outline should contain the following:

- an introduction stating the topic of the paper
- the main points that support the topic (often labeled with Roman numerals)
- supporting ideas for each major point (often labeled with capital letters)
- subdivisions of supporting ideas, if needed (often labeled with Arabic numerals)
- supporting graphics such as a data table, a graph, a map, or art, if appropriate
- a conclusion

The Lesson

Introduce: Using the information above, explain to students what an outline is. Then distribute a copy of page 45 to each student and have them read the scenario. Discuss it, asking students if they've ever planned out a paper before writing it.

Look at a Model: Have students read the model writing sample, "My Favorite Holiday." Discuss it, asking students if they can tell how the paper will be organized and written. Ask if the student seems to have an organized plan for her writing. Ask whether they think anything could be added or changed in Clara's outline.

Analyze the Model: Distribute a copy of the graphic organizer on page 46 to each student. Guide students through finding the information in the model writing sample to complete the graphic organizer. Some parts of the graphic organizer may not apply.

Write: Assign and provide copies of one or both writing tasks on pages 47 and 48 or let students choose. Also provide copies of the graphic organizer. Make sure students understand the task before beginning. If needed, brainstorm ideas as a class to complete the graphic organizer. Then have students write their outlines.

Extend: If desired, have students brainstorm types of writing in their own lives in which it may be useful to write an outline first, such as a speech for a ceremony or a persuasive request. Have them complete the extension activity on page 48 on a separate sheet of paper.

Name ______________________________

Organizing Your Thoughts

Clara's class was asked to write a paper about their favorite holiday. This is the outline Clara wrote to plan her paper.

My Favorite Holiday

Topic: My favorite holiday

Purpose: Inform (personal essay)

Introduction: Thanksgiving is my favorite

I. Family
   A. Cousins visit!
   B. Uncle Joe always brings presents

II. Food—show photo of last year's meal
   A. Sweet potatoes with marshmallows on top!
   B. Stuffing
   C. Pumpkin pie
   D. I get to help cook

III. Vacation
   A. A whole week off from school!
   B. Travel
      1. Sledding at Grandma's
      2. Amusement park
   C. Video games

Conclusion

Name ____________________

Outline Graphic Organizer

Introduction of topic

I (main point)

A (supporting detail)

B (supporting detail)

II (main point)

A (supporting detail)

B (supporting detail)

III (main point)

A (supporting detail)

B (supporting detail)

Conclusion

Name ____________________

The Best Day Writing Task #1

Imagine that your teacher gave you an assignment to write a paper about the best day of your life. Start your paper with an introduction statement such as, "The best day of my life was ________." The main points in your outline will be the best parts of the day. The supporting details in your outline will be descriptions of those best parts, which will help explain why they were so great.

Name ___________________________

Renewable Energy Writing Task #2

Imagine that you are writing a report about using renewable energy for a class assignment. Research green energy options and decide which type would work best where you live. Then write an outline for your report.

Extension Activity

Think of a time in your life when you will need to prepare a speech. For example, you might need to speak at a ceremony such as a bar mitzvah or bat mitzvah or persuade your parents to increase your allowance. Write an outline of what you would say in your speech.

Weighing In

Reviews have become a powerful consumer tool that can make or break the success of a product, service, or piece of art or entertainment. Most business websites offer a Reviews page that shows customers' past experiences with the product or service. Independent review sites, such as Yelp and the Better Business Bureau, let people give their honest thoughts. People also post opinions on their own social media pages.

Anyone looking for advice on where to stay on vacation or which gymnastics school to enroll in now has plenty of advice, especially when a review is clearly written.

A review should contain the following:

- a clearly stated opinion
- facts that specifically describe what is being reviewed
- examples and details that support stated opinions
- specific and respectful language, especially when expressing negative emotions
- a recommendation statement
- pictures that support the critique, if appropriate

The Lesson

Introduce: Using the information above, explain to students what a retail product or service review is. Then distribute a copy of page 50 to each student and have them read the scenario. Discuss it, asking students what kinds of positive and negative experiences they have had buying new items.

Look at a Model: Have students read the model writing sample, "Backpack looks better than it works." Discuss it, asking students if the writer's thoughts are clear. Have students summarize the review. Ask whether they think anything could be added or changed to make the writer's thoughts more clear or relevant.

Analyze the Model: Distribute a copy of the graphic organizer on page 51 to each student. Guide students through finding the information in the model writing sample to complete the graphic organizer. Some parts of the graphic organizer may not apply.

Write: Assign and provide copies of one or both writing tasks on pages 52 and 53 or let students choose. Also provide copies of the graphic organizer. Make sure students understand the task before beginning. If needed, brainstorm ideas as a class to complete the graphic organizer. Then have students write their reviews.

Extend: If desired, have students brainstorm some additional products, services, or other experiences that they want to analyze and share their thoughts about. Have them complete the extension activity on page 53 on a separate sheet of paper.

Product Review

Amir got a new backpack at the start of the school year. He had used his previous backpack for two years, and it was starting to wear out. Also, he joined the track team, so now he needs to carry running shoes and a water bottle. Amir and his parents went to several stores to look at backpacks, and he finally chose one.

Amir has been using his new backpack for one month. He has written an online review on the website for the store that sold it.

Backpack looks better than it works ★★☆☆☆

I bought a new backpack for the start of 5th grade. The one I got in 3rd grade was starting to wear out. A hole was forming in two spots.

We went to three stores. I brought my old one with all my stuff in it to make sure everything would fit inside the new one. I finally found one I liked at Hilliard's Hiking. It is black and has pictures of sports balls on it. Everyone at school thought it was cool.

After the first couple of weeks, I couldn't find any pencils in it. When I took everything out, I saw that it already had a hole in the bottom! I had to get a separate case for my pencils. When track practice began, I needed to carry a water bottle, but it wouldn't fit in the outside bottle pocket. And the added weight of my track shoes is making one strap tear already! 😫 I'm disappointed in this backpack and would not recommend it.

Name ______________________________

Review Graphic Organizer

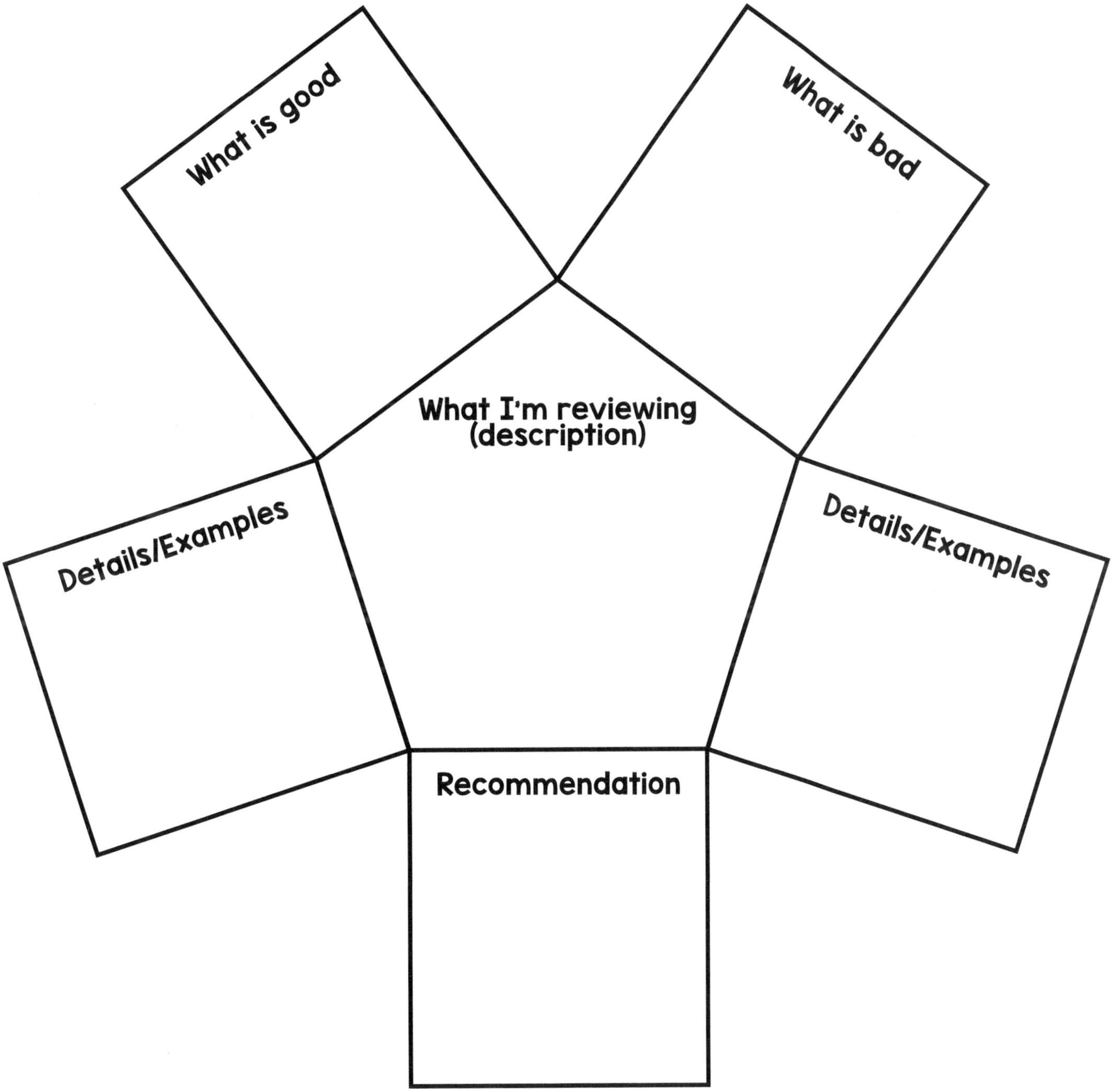

Name ______________________________

Restaurant Review Writing Task #1

Imagine that your cousins are in town and they want to know of a good place to eat breakfast. Write a review of a good breakfast diner for them. Include a picture of the diner or a meal.

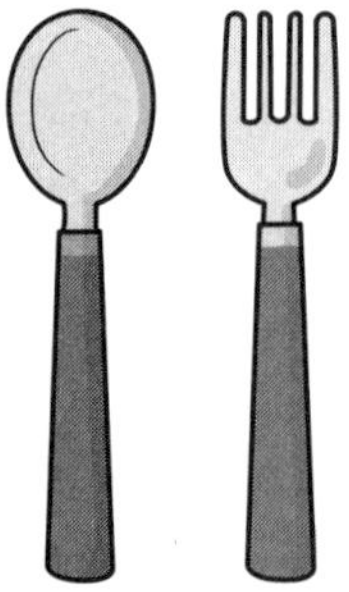

Name ____________________

Medical Care Review Writing Task #2

Think about the doctor, nurse, or medical clinic that you visit if you are sick or hurt. Write a review for people who are new to your neighborhood.

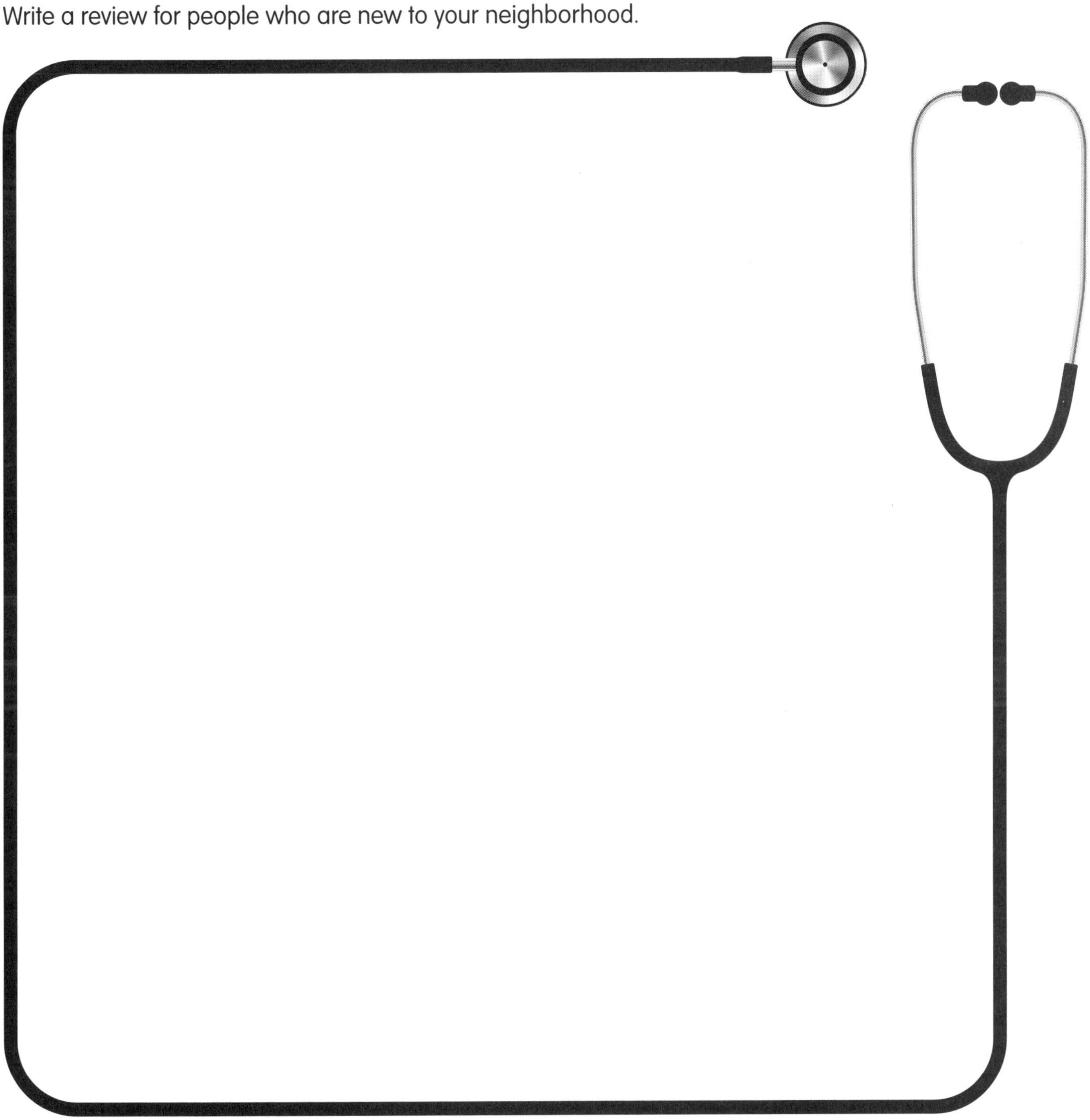

Extension Activity

Think of a product or service you have used. What did you think about it? Write a review to let other people know what you thought and whether they should spend money on it.

Peer Review

Many teachers have students do a peer review of each other's work as part of the learning process in all subjects. Feedback from one student to another can help strengthen student work and can be less intimidating. Peer review has other benefits as well, such as giving students a chance to think about a topic more critically, seeing the effect of different approaches to an assignment, getting another perspective, identifying strengths and weaknesses in their own thinking, and helping students be more engaged with their class.

Many students are understandably nervous about peer reviews. It is stressful for students to have classmates read their work. It may also make students anxious to give criticism to other students, who might take it personally. It is important for students to focus their comments on the *writing,* not the *writer.*

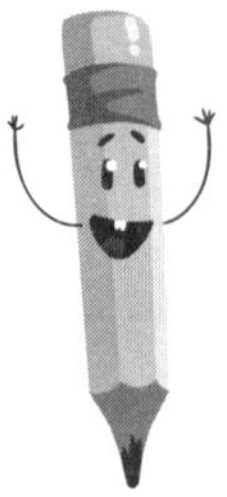

An effective peer review should contain the following:

- positive comments about the work
- explanations of specific errors or vague or disorganized thoughts
- suggestions for making changes
- different types of feedback (proofreading, structure, focus, creativity)
- language that is kind, respectful, and supportive

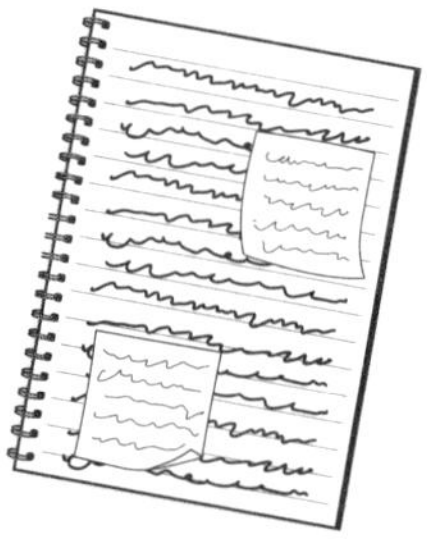

The Lesson

Introduce: Using the information above, explain to students what peer feedback is. Then distribute a copy of page 55 to each student and have them read the scenario. Discuss it, asking students what kinds of positive and negative experiences they have had with reviewing other students' work or receiving reviews from other students.

Look at a Model: Have students read the model writing sample, "Eli's Essay." Discuss it, asking students how they think Eli would respond. Have students point out examples of useful comments and helpful language. Ask whether they think anything could be added or changed in the peer review.

Analyze the Model: Distribute a copy of the graphic organizer on page 56 to each student. Guide students through finding the information in the model writing sample to complete the graphic organizer. Some parts of the graphic organizer may not apply.

Write: Assign and provide copies of one or both writing tasks on pages 57 and 58 or let students choose. Also provide copies of the graphic organizer. Make sure students understand the task before beginning. If needed, brainstorm ideas as a class to complete the graphic organizer. Then have students write their reviews of the student work.

Extend: If desired, have students brainstorm situations in their own lives in which they may have the experience, expertise, or perspective needed to review someone's work. Have them complete the extension activity on page 58 on a separate sheet of paper.

Making an Argument

Miriam's class had to write an essay for school. Her classmate, Eli, chose the topic "Given the dangers of smoking, should cigarettes be outlawed?"

Miriam's teacher paired up students for peer reviews. Miriam and Eli reviewed each other's essays. Here is Eli's essay along with Miriam's comments.

Eli's Essay

I think cigerettes should be outlawed. They smell bad and they are bad for your health. Every year, thousands of people die from lung cancer that they got from smoking. Besides lung cancer, people get other kinds of cancer from smoking, like mouth cancer and throat cancer, plus people get heart problems from smoking.

Another reason cigerettes should be outlawed is because they are bad for other people's health. When one person smokes, other people breathe that smoke, and that is not healthy for them either.

Some people are addicted and that will make it super hard to quit when it's outlawed. But maybe that will be the push they need to finally quit. My grandpa was addicted to smoking and he died young. My mom was always sad about that. Outlawing smoking would have made my mom a lot happier since she might still have her dad around even now.

Miriam's comments:

- Fix spelling. (cigerettes, first paragraph)
- I think you should move this to the second paragraph. That is where you talk about how cigarettes bother others. (They smell bad)
- Fix run-on. Break into two sentences. (Besides lung cancer, … heart problems from smoking.)
- Fix spelling. (cigerettes, second paragraph)
- This is a great paragraph with this powerful example that supports your main point that cigarettes should be outlawed. Nice job! (My grandpa was addicted … always sad about that.)

Name ______________________________

Peer Review Graphic Organizer

What I am reviewing

Suggestion 1

Suggestion 2

Suggestion 3

Great job on this:

Name ____________________

Newspaper Entry Writing Task #1

Imagine that your school newspaper is publishing an article on different ways students spent their summer break. The editor is asking for entries from students. Your twin sister wrote this entry for the article and asked for your thoughts. Read the entry and write feedback for her.

What I Did on Summer Break

I had fun. At the beginning of the summer we visited my granma and grampa. At the end of the summer we went to Disneyland. When we went there, we went to a hotel with a pool I played in the pool alot with my brother and sister. The pool was really fun. My granma and granpa's house was fun too cause they have a big dog named Rover that I like to play with. Granma always makes us chocolate chip pancakes for breakfast my favorite. Summer is fun because there's no school and we go lots of places and have fun.

Name ______________________________

Contest Writing Task #2

Imagine that your classmate wrote this essay for a Women's History Month essay contest. You've been asked to review it. Read the essay and then write helpful comments.

The Life and Accomplishments of Marie Curie

Marie Curie was a famous sientist. She was born in Poland in 1867. She died in France in 1934 when she was 66 years old. She probably died from radiation from her sientific work.

When Marie was born her name was Maria Salomea Skłodowska. Her parents were teachers and her dad taught her a lot of stuff. She wasn't allowed to go to college in Poland because she was a girl.

Marie liked chemistry. Even though she loved Poland, she moved to France so that she could work in a lab as a chemist. She met a man named Pierre Curie. He liked chemistry too. They got married. Then they became famous for their discoveries about radioactivity. They won a Nobel Prize in Physics, which is a very important sience prize. Then her husband died. She kept working and won another Nobel Prize. The second one was in Chemistry. Marie Curie is the only person ever to win two Nobel Prizes in two different areas of sience.

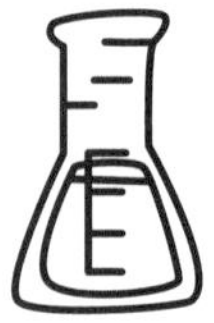

Marie Curie probably died from her work. When she first studied radioactivity, no one new it was dangerous. So she didn't protect herself like we do now. That's probably why she died. Her daughter won a Nobel Prize too.

Extension Activity

Ask a classmate, your brother or sister, or a friend if he or she is working on a school assignment or a real-world project and would like feedback from you. It could be a writing assignment, a math problem, a science project, or a community flier, but it should be something that you know about. Write helpful comments and suggestions about the work.

Critique Carefully | **Media Review**

That's Entertainment (or Not)

In the days before the Internet, only professional critics wrote reviews of movies, books, music recordings, and other forms of art and entertainment, collectively known as **media**. Today, anyone can write a review and post it online. The public's recommendations are helpful to the public, as others like to see what people "just like them" think, rather than only the opinion of a professional critic. Also, with so many reviews, audiences get a clearer sense of whether it's worth it to spend their money and time on the entertainment.

Some review websites, such as Metacritic and imdb, have a Users' Reviews section that shows viewers' opinions of shows and movies. People also post reviews on their own social media pages. Some even start review blogs or vlogs.

A media review should contain the following:

- the title of the review
- a statement of what you are reviewing (its title and the type of media)
- a brief summary of the work that doesn't give away any plot surprises
- your overall opinion
- details of aspects you liked and didn't like with supporting examples
- a rating, if applicable to the review forum

The Lesson

Introduce: Using the information above, explain to students what a media review is. Then distribute a copy of page 60 to each student and have them read the scenario. Discuss it, asking students if they like every book, show, and movie they come across or if they dislike some, or if they sometimes like some parts but not other parts of the same work.

Look at a Model: Have students read the model writing sample, "Great for 4-year-olds, but..." Discuss it, asking students if the writer's opinions are clear. Have students summarize the review. Ask whether they think anything could be added or changed to make the writer's thoughts more clear or relevant.

Analyze the Model: Distribute a copy of the graphic organizer on page 61 to each student. Guide students through finding the information in the model writing sample to complete the graphic organizer. Some parts of the graphic organizer may not apply.

Write: Assign and provide copies of one or both writing tasks on pages 62 and 63 or let students choose. Also provide copies of the graphic organizer. Make sure students understand the task before beginning. If needed, brainstorm ideas as a class to complete the graphic organizer. Then have students write their reviews.

Extend: If desired, have students brainstorm some additional books, shows, or other forms of entertainment that they want to share their thoughts about. Have them complete the extension activity on page 63 on a separate sheet of paper.

TV Show Review

Kingston babysat his 4-year-old brother, Benji. Together they watched a few episodes of Benji's favorite show. Kingston wrote an online review of the show. The review is on a popular website that encourages members of the public to review television shows.

Great for 4-year-olds, but... ★★★★☆

My brother and I watched the TV show Firefighter Flamingoes. It's about a bunch of flamingoes that race to put out fires at the zoo. Benji thought it was hilarious. He was on the edge of his seat, wondering if they were going to put out the fire and save the day.

I was glad Benji liked it, since it's made for kids his age. But it's not entertaining for an older babysitter to watch. I was really bored. The humor isn't for anyone older than 4 or 5 years old. The animation was pretty good, but the music was totally annoying.

I'm giving this show 4 stars, since my brother loved it. But I'm leaving off one star because it isn't interesting for anyone older who has to watch it with a little kid.

Name ______________________________

Media Review Graphic Organizer

Title of review

Parts that are good

What I'm reviewing

What it's about

Parts that could be better

Overall opinion

☆☆☆☆☆

Name ______________________________

Skip This Show! Writing Task #1

Think about the last movie or play that you watched that you **didn't** like.
Write a review of the show for the show's website.

Name ____________________

Book Review Writing Task #2

Think about a book that you read. Consider things about it that you liked as well as what you didn't like. Write a review of the book for someone who is thinking of reading it.

Extension Activity

Think of a book that you read, a movie or a TV show that you saw, or a music video that you listened to. Read reviews of it online and then add your own review. Do not give any personal information in the review, such as your full name or where you live. Make sure that your parent or guardian reads your review **before** you post it.

Everyone's a Critic

The Internet contains a wealth of information and entertainment. Anyone with online access can research any topic, learn a new skill, consult with others about a hobby or an interest, buy anything, share a talent, and chat with friends. There are also many sites that range from boring to ridiculous to dangerous. While it is important to shelter students from some sites, it is equally important to help them learn to evaluate the material they come across and respond to it appropriately.

Many articles and videos online have a section for comments where members of the public can write something. The Comments section can be a valuable way to gather people's reactions and opinions. Some people give positive feedback. Others offer another viewpoint. Comments are also a way for people who don't know each other to have a conversation about a topic that they share an interest in.

An online comment about an article or a video should contain the following:

- a statement of support for or disagreement with the article or video
- a clearly stated opinion or point of view
- something that hasn't already been stated, if possible
- an example or additional information, if appropriate
- polite and respectful language, especially if expressing disagreement

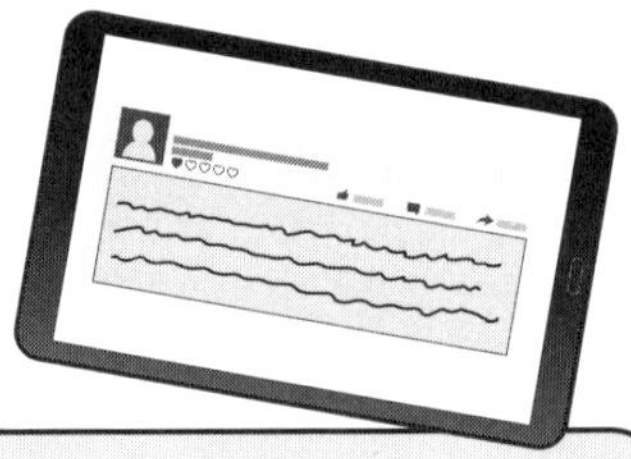

The Lesson

Introduce: Using the information above, explain to students what an online comment is. Then distribute a copy of page 65 to each student and have them read the scenario and the opinion article, "Length of the School Day." Discuss it, asking students if they have ever read an article or an opinion letter online. Ask if they agree or disagree with the School Day article. Ask if they have ever noticed, read, or responded to any comments about an article or an opinion letter.

Look at a Model: Have students read the model writing sample, "Jacob's Response." Discuss it, asking students if they felt Jacob's comment added anything valuable to the post and why. Ask whether they think anything could be added or changed to make the comment clearer.

Analyze the Model: Distribute a copy of the graphic organizer on page 66 to each student. Guide students through finding the information in the model writing sample to complete the graphic organizer. Some parts of the graphic organizer may not apply.

Write: Assign and provide copies of one or both writing tasks on pages 67 and 68 or let students choose. Also provide copies of the graphic organizer. Make sure students understand the task before beginning. If needed, brainstorm ideas as a class to complete the graphic organizer. Then have students write their comments.

Extend: If desired, have students brainstorm online sites that they visit to which they could contribute a comment to the online conversation. Have them complete the extension activity on page 68 on a separate sheet of paper.

School Day Length Debate

Jacob read the following online opinion article entitled "Length of the School Day." Jacob didn't agree with the writer, so he used the Comments section to explain his viewpoint.

Length of the School Day

by Rachel Doe

Right now, students attend school from about 8:30 a.m. until 3:00 p.m. Monday through Friday. The start and end times are slightly different at different schools, but that's about right. Most adults work from about 8:00 a.m. until 5:00 p.m. So there are a couple of hours in the afternoon when younger kids need to have supervision.

Meanwhile, the newspapers say that students aren't doing well enough in school. The answer seems obvious to me: make the school day longer. If kids went to school two hours longer, they would learn more. Plus, they wouldn't need additional supervision in the late afternoon because their teachers would be watching them.

Jacob's Response

I see what you mean about parents needing after-school supervision for their kids. But I don't think you have the solution. As a sixth grader, I can tell you that kids get tired and won't learn during the extra two hours. Plus, kids need time to run and play or do art. I'm sure you're right that kids need to do better in school. But a longer school day isn't the answer.

Name ____________________

Online Comment Graphic Organizer

Statement of support or disagreement

↓

Commentor's opinion

↓

New points, examples, or additional information

Name ______________________________

Dance Video Writing Task #1

Imagine that you just watched an online video of someone doing a hip-hop dance in his or her home. There are already some comments. Write your own comment in the Comments section.

★★★★★

Great moves! I like this old song.
She sure can keep the beat!

★☆☆☆☆

I've seen better. She couldn't
compete on a dance show.

☆☆☆☆☆

Name ____________________

Chores Article Writing Task #2

Imagine that you read an online article about kids having too many chores. Write a comment.

User Name

270 REPLY

View 32 replies

Extension Activity

Find an online article or video. Leave a public comment. Do not give any personal information in the comment such as your full name or where you live. Make sure that your parent or guardian reads your comment **before** you post it.

Dive in Deep | **Request Letter**

I Have a Request

We ask for things every day, usually from family, classmates, teachers, friends, and colleagues. Usually, we are asking for something that is easy to provide: a quick answer, a little help, or an item that is easy to get. We can ask someone in person or pick up the phone. But sometimes we need something from people who don't live nearby or even from people we don't know. Sometimes we need something unusual or something we're not comfortable asking for. In these cases, it might be better to write a letter or an e-mail to make a request.

A request letter should contain the following:

- a greeting to a specific person, if possible
- an introduction, if writing to someone you don't know
- a clear description of what you are asking for
- the reason for your request
- the time frame in which you need whatever was requested
- a closing with your name and contact information
- formal and polite language
- correct spelling, grammar, and punctuation

The Lesson

Introduce: Using the information above, explain to students what a request letter is. Then distribute a copy of page 70 to each student and have them read the scenario. Discuss it, asking students how they think Abdullah feels as he writes the message and how Ms. Chan might feel as she reads it. Ask when it might be better to make a request in writing rather than in person.

Look at a Model: Have students read the model writing sample, "Requesting a Do-Over." Discuss it, asking students what is being requested, why, and how they would respond to the request. Ask whether they think anything could be added or changed to improve the request.

Analyze the Model: Distribute a copy of the graphic organizer on page 71 to each student. Guide students through finding the information in the model writing sample to complete the graphic organizer. Some parts of the graphic organizer may not apply.

Write: Assign and provide copies of one or both writing tasks on pages 72 and 73 or let students choose. Also provide copies of the graphic organizer. Make sure students understand the task before beginning. If needed, brainstorm ideas as a class to complete the graphic organizer. Then have students write their request letters.

Extend: If desired, have students brainstorm situations in their own lives in which they might need to write a request letter. Have them complete the extension activity on page 73 on a separate sheet of paper.

Can I Try Again?

Abdullah was not happy about how he did on his math test. He sent an e-mail to his teacher requesting a retest. Below is his letter of request.

New Message

To Ms. Chan

Subject **Requesting a Do-Over**

Dear Ms. Chan,

I know I didn't do well on the math test we just took on Friday. I am writing to ask if I can take a retest.

I was really having trouble adding and subtracting fractions. I planned to review how to do that on Thursday night. But then I came home super tired from baseball practice on Thursday afternoon, and I fell asleep without studying. I know I shouldn't have left studying until the night before. I won't do that in the future. But over the weekend, I went over homework problems that I'd messed up before. I figured out what I was doing wrong and did those problems again. My grandmother checked my work and said they are correct now.

Report cards come out next week, so I know there is not much time. Would it be possible for me to come in early any day this week to take the test again?

Respectfully,

Abdullah Ghali

SEND

Name ______________________________

Request Letter Graphic Organizer

Greeting

Self-introduction (if needed)

What is being requested

Reason for request

Time frame

Closing

Name ______________________________

Camping Fundraiser Writing Task #1

Imagine that you are in a Scout troop that needs to raise money to go on a camping trip. Your troop has decided to have an online auction to raise money. At an auction, buyers bid money for any items they want to buy. The person with the highest bid on an item gets to buy it. Each troop member has to ask someone to donate an item. You are asking your trumpet teacher to donate a gift certificate for two free trumpet lessons. Write the letter to your trumpet teacher.

Name ______________________________

Gym Sports Writing Task #2

Imagine that you want a new sport offered during gym class, such as dance, table tennis, golf, tae kwon do, archery, or badminton. Write an e-mail to the physical education department requesting that they add the sport that you suggest.

To ______________________________

Subject ______________________________

Extension Activity

Think of something you would like to request, such as asking a family member for information about your ancestors or asking a summer music camp how you can try out for it. Write a letter and send a copy of it. Make sure your parent or guardian reviews the letter **before** you send it.

Survey Says...

Surveys are valuable tools that gather data to help people make decisions. Survey results help everyone from individual people to large organizations focus their time, energy, and money in useful ways. Surveys can tell us what the public likes or dislikes about different brands of products, how to improve a company's service, what kinds of classes a community center should offer, or which candidate people are likely to vote for in an election.

Surveys may be given online, by phone, via e-mail, through the postal mail, or in person. There are different types of questions, such as multiple-choice, yes/no, a rating scale, and short written answers. A survey can use just one of these types of questions or a combination of question types.

A survey should contain the following:

- the reason for the survey
- instructions for marking answers and returning the survey
- questions that all support the goal or purpose of the survey
- a neutral tone to avoid influencing responses
- clear, simple wording

The Lesson

Introduce: Using the information above, explain to students what a survey is. Then distribute a copy of page 75 to each student and have them read the scenario. Discuss it, asking students if they like giving their opinions about things. Ask how J'Nelle might use the information she collects.

Look at a Model: Have students read the model writing sample, "Student Council Survey." Discuss it, asking why J'Nelle used different formats for different questions. Ask students if everything seems unbiased. Ask whether they think anything could be added or changed to improve the survey.

Analyze the Model: Distribute a copy of the graphic organizer on page 76 to each student. Guide students through finding the information in the model writing sample to complete the graphic organizer. Some parts of the graphic organizer may not apply.

Write: Assign and provide copies of one or both writing tasks on pages 77 and 78 or let students choose. Also provide copies of the graphic organizer. Make sure students understand the task before beginning. If needed, brainstorm ideas as a class to complete the graphic organizer. Then have students write their survey questions.

Extend: If desired, have students brainstorm situations in their own lives in which they might need or want to write a survey. Have them complete the extension activity on page 78 on a separate sheet of paper.

Polling: What Student Council Needs to Do

J'Nelle is helping a friend who is running for student council president. She wants to know who might win as well as what is most important to students right now. She wrote the survey below.

Student Council Survey

This survey is to find out who might win student council elections and why.

Directions: Skip any questions that you do not want to answer. Do **not** write your name on the survey. Leave your survey in the box in the office.

1. On the scale shown, circle how you think student council did last year.

2. Circle the student you hope will be the next student council president.

   A. Enrique
   B. David
   C. Zahara
   D. Mandeep
   E. undecided
   F. no one

3. Why are you planning to vote for the person you chose?

   A. I like his/her campaign posters.
   B. He/She gave a great speech.
   C. He/She will do something that I'm in favor of.
   D. I am his/her friend.
   E. I don't like the other candidates.
   F. other (explain) ______________________________

4. What would you **most** like your student council to do this year?

____

____

Name ______________________________

Survey Graphic Organizer

Survey purpose

Instructions for marking

Instructions for returning

Question 1	**Question 2**
Question 3	**Question 4**

Checklist

- ❑ Questions are neutral and unbiased.
- ❑ Wording is clear.
- ❑ There are enough answer options.

Name ______________________________

Exercise Survey Writing Task #1

Imagine that you are doing a project to help make physical education classes more popular. Write a survey to find out how much kids your age exercise, what types of exercise they prefer, and if they think exercise is important.

Survey Title:

Name ____________________

Recycling Survey Writing Task #2

Imagine that the recycling bins at your school are not being used very much. Create a survey for the students and adults at your school to gather information. Try to determine which groups are not using the bins: Teachers or students? Male or female? Which grades? Also try to find out why they are not using them and what might improve their use.

Survey Title:

Extension Activity

Think of something you would like to find out with a survey. It could relate to what people buy, such as clothing; their attitude toward an issue such as safe air and water; or how they are affected by a problem such as bullying. Give the survey to people and tally the results. Make sure that your parent or guardian reviews the survey and your plan for sending it and collecting responses **before** you send it out.

Information, Please

Perhaps students are looking for summer work as a camp counselor or want to volunteer at a local food bank. While students might not find any openings for a job or a volunteer position, that shouldn't stop them from contacting an organization that they are interested in. Sending an inquiry letter is an opportunity for self-marketing. The letter shows personality and passion for the type of work. It shows that the writer takes initiative and is an active learner.

Students don't have to wait until they are old enough to work to send an inquiry letter. Some organizations hold career days to excite future workers about what they do and to guide them toward useful classes. Some offer internships that give students a valuable glimpse into what certain jobs look like. Some organizations will give informational interviews to explain different aspects of the work. These are all things that can be asked about in an inquiry letter.

An inquiry letter should contain the following:

- a greeting to a specific person, if possible
- the reason you are writing
- the type of job you are interested in
- a description of experiences you have had that might use similar skills
- your contact information, the date, a greeting, a closing, and your signature
- formal and polite language with correct spelling, grammar, and punctuation

The Lesson

Introduce: Using the information above, explain to students what an inquiry letter is. Then distribute a copy of page 80 to each student and have them read the scenario. Discuss it, asking students what Muriel could learn from working at the animal shelter.

Look at a Model: Have students read the model writing sample, "Tell Me More." Discuss it, asking students how they think Mr. Esquivel would react to Muriel's letter. Ask whether they think anything could be added or changed to improve the letter.

Analyze the Model: Distribute a copy of the graphic organizer on page 81 to each student. Guide students through finding the information in the model writing sample to complete the graphic organizer. Some parts of the graphic organizer may not apply.

Write: Assign and provide copies of one or both writing tasks on pages 82 and 83 or let students choose. Also provide copies of the graphic organizer. Make sure students understand the task before beginning. If needed, brainstorm ideas as a class to complete the graphic organizer. Then have students write their letters.

Extend: If desired, have students brainstorm situations in their own lives in which writing an inquiry letter may be useful in the future. Have them complete the extension activity on page 83 on a separate sheet of paper.

How Can I Help You?

Muriel loves the outdoors and animals. She would like to train guide dogs someday or maybe run an animal sanctuary. Muriel thought that volunteering at an animal shelter would give her useful and interesting experience. She wrote a letter to the manager of her local animal shelter.

Tell Me More

123 Canid Street, Apt. 2B
Wooferton, UT 84099

March 9, 2022

Dear Mr. Esquivel,

My name is Muriel and I'm in 6th grade. I love animals, and I am thinking about a career in animal care when I'm older. I have had a pet hamster for a year, and I take great care of it. I love all animals and am passionate about caring for them. I do volunteer dog-walking for senior citizens in my neighborhood.

I was wondering if I can volunteer at the shelter. I can feed animals, clean up after them, play with them, and give them exercise and attention. I'm really organized. I can make sure that all the toys, leashes, and bowls are put away correctly. I also want to learn about other shelter jobs and what kind of training they require.

The shelter is only two blocks from my school, so I could volunteer after school any day of the week. If you are interested, please contact me at MurielTheAnimalLover@me.com. I look forward to hearing from you!

Sincerely,

Muriel Williams

Muriel Williams

Name ______________________________

Inquiry Letter Graphic Organizer

Address of sender:

Today's Date:

Greeting:

Body of letter:

Introduction

Background

Request

Contact

Closing:

Signature:

Typed Name:

Name ______________________________

Internship Letter Writing Task #1

Imagine that you have a neighbor who works for a video game company. She lets you try out games that are being created. You would like to learn what it takes to design video games. Your neighbor mentioned that the company uses student interns to come up with new game ideas. Interns work for six months without pay doing small tasks alongside employees. Write a letter to find out more about how to become an intern.

Name ______________________________

Lifeguard Letter Writing Task #2

Imagine that the lifeguard at your community pool is moving away to go to college. You have had lifeguard training and passed a course in first aid. Write an inquiry letter to the Parks and Recreation Department introducing yourself and asking if a new lifeguard has been chosen yet.

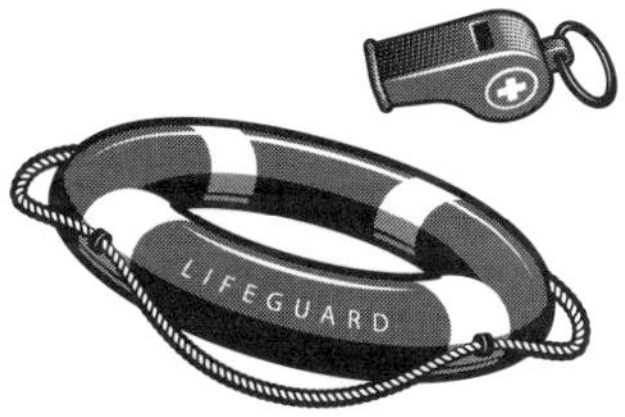

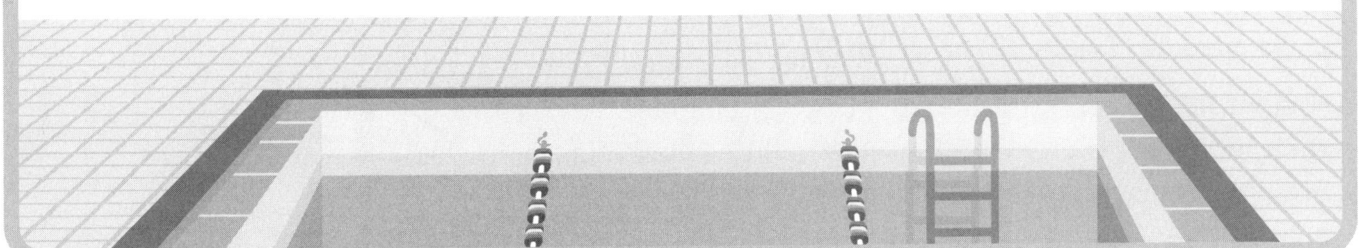

Extension Activity

Think of a job you would like to have in the future. Write an inquiry letter. You can include some experience that you plan to have by the time you could train for or apply for that job. Make up contact information instead of using your real information.

Dive in Deep | **Quiz-Game Questions**

Know and Win

Most people enjoy a quiz game. It gives them a chance to show off their knowledge of trivia and to learn interesting things. Plus, many people enjoy friendly competition. Constructing a game can be fun and even helpful to prepare for a test. However, the questions must also be fun and interesting for the players so they don't become bored or annoyed.

Give your game a fun and inviting title. Use a wide range of topics and a mixture of difficulty levels so that there is something for everyone. Decide on the rules and format of your game before writing your questions. Does each player draw a question card one at a time and try to answer it, or is there a game leader reading the questions for all players to try to answer? How are points scored? What happens when someone answers incorrectly? Is there a way to contest a wrong answer that a player thinks is correct?

Quiz-game questions should contain the following:

- topics that your audience is familiar with
- interesting facts; don't ask opinion questions
- a hint or clue to help players figure it out
- one and only one correct answer
- answer options (in multiple-choice) that sound possible but aren't
- up-to-date information verified by reliable sources

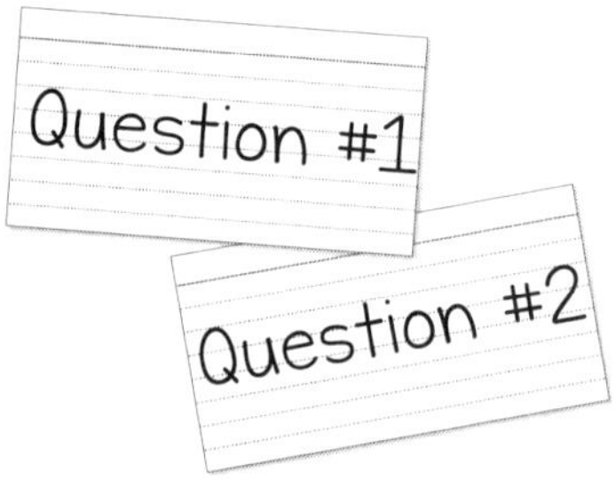

The Lesson

Introduce: Using the information above, explain to students what a quiz game is. Then distribute a copy of page 85 to each student and have them read the scenario. Discuss it, asking students to compare answering questions in a game to answering questions in class. Ask if they have ever used a quiz game to study and how well it worked.

Look at a Model: Have students read the model writing sample, "Who's the Animal Genius Among Us?" Discuss it, asking students which were their favorite questions and why. Ask whether they think anything could be added or changed to improve the questions.

Analyze the Model: Distribute a copy of the graphic organizer on page 86 to each student. Guide students through finding the information in the model writing sample to complete the graphic organizer. Some parts of the graphic organizer may not apply.

Write: Assign and provide copies of one or both writing tasks on pages 87 and 88 or let students choose. Also provide copies of the graphic organizer. Make sure students understand the task before beginning. If needed, brainstorm ideas as a class to complete the graphic organizer. Then have students write their quiz-game questions.

Extend: If desired, have students brainstorm situations in their own lives in which they might want to write quiz-game questions. Have them complete the extension activity on page 88 on a separate sheet of paper.

Animal Quiz Game

Yael is writing a quiz game for family game night at her middle school. Parents and students from 11 to 15 years old will participate. Yael knows that some students love animals, soccer, video games, and chess. The school mascot is a lion, so she is giving her quiz game an animal theme. She is creating a mix of multiple-choice and true-or-false questions. Here are some of the questions she wrote.

Who's the Animal Genius Among Us?

1. Giant pandas have black patches around their eyes, making them look like cuddly toys. What country is the native habitat of the giant panda?

   a. China *
   b. Kenya
   c. Canada
   d. India

2. A mammal holds the record for being the largest animal ever. What is that mammal?

   a. giganotosaurus
   b. woolly mammoth
   c. blue whale *
   d. elephant

3. Which of the following are scorpions, mites, and ticks related to?

   a. caterpillars
   b. spiders *
   c. bees
   d. insects

4. Which African plant eater has the heaviest heart of any land mammal?

   a. horse
   b. elephant *
   c. hippo
   d. giraffe

5. True or false: Pink flamingoes are pink because they eat shrimp.

   a. true *
   b. false

Name ____________________

Quiz-Game Graphic Organizer

Who is my audience?

Name of quiz game

Format of game or question

Possible topic 1

Possible topic 2

Possible topic 3

Question

Answer or answer choices (put a * next to the correct choice)

Checklist

- ❑ accurate
- ❑ interesting
- ❑ has only one answer

Source for checking the answer: ____________________

Name ______________________________

Sports Quiz Writing Task #1

Imagine that your sports team is having a celebration night. Each player has been asked to write one question for a quiz game that will be part of the entertainment at the celebration. Choose any sport you are familiar with, such as basketball, swimming, table tennis, soccer, track, gymnastics, ice hockey, skateboarding, or skiing. Write a quiz-game question for that sport.

Sport:

 Name ____________________

Class Review Writing Task #2

Imagine that you have a test coming up. To review for the test, your teacher has told each student to write a quiz-game question about the material. You will play the game in class, using the students' questions. Choose a topic you have been learning about in class (science or social studies are good subjects for finding interesting questions). Write a quiz-game question for your topic.

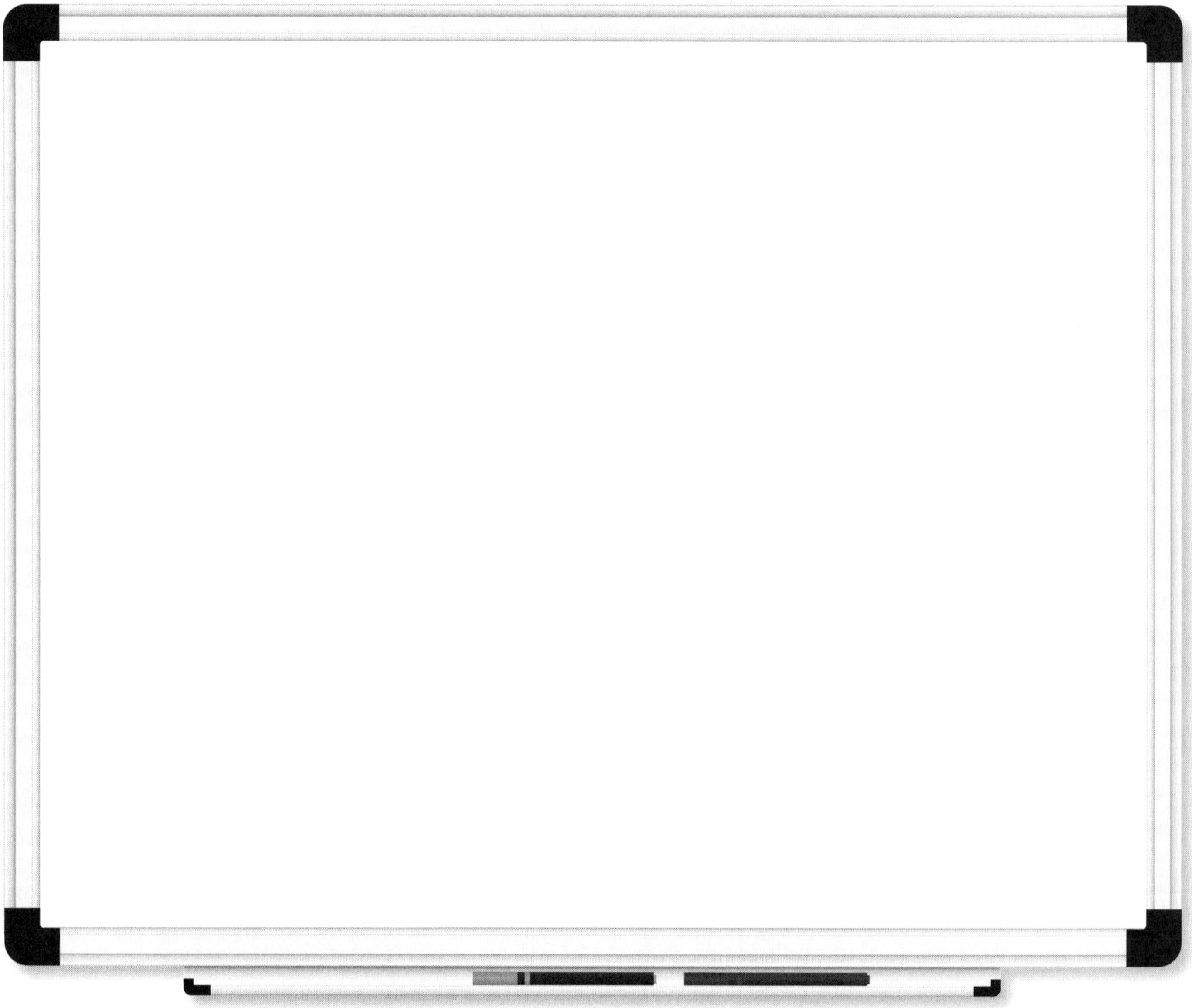

Extension Activity

Think of a group that would enjoy playing a quiz game. For example, your friends might like questions about a favorite TV show, your family could answer questions about your vacation location, or a club could use questions to learn about the club's history. Write ten questions for the quiz game. Then play the quiz game with the group.

Information Hunters

Print, radio, television, and online journalism require meaningful reporting. No matter how the public accesses it—reading a newspaper or magazine, listening to radio, watching TV, or reading or streaming on a screen—the audience expects accurate, useful information. They want to know about major events far and near, the weather, health news, local crimes, scientific breakthroughs, scandals, sports and entertainment celebrities, and human-interest stories. People may prefer some types of reports over others, but everyone needs to connect with society.

Reporters are the people who bring us breaking information. They ask questions, find data, dig for clues, figure out which information is most important for their audience, and then present it.

A news report should contain the following:

- a clearly stated focus
- facts about the topic
- multiple perspectives from everyone involved or affected
- objective, unbiased language
- empathy for anyone negatively affected
- correct grammar, spelling, and punctuation
- pictures or graphics that clarify the story or its impact

The Lesson

Introduce: Using the information above, explain to students what a news report is. Then distribute a copy of page 90 to each student and have them read the scenario. Discuss it, asking students how they learn about what goes on in the world around them. Ask what kinds of information are important to them and what shows, websites, or articles they access.

Look at a Model: Have students read the model writing sample, "Peacocks Come to School." Discuss it, asking students if the report is clear and if they found it interesting and why. Ask whether they think anything could be added or changed to make the report more objective or clear.

Analyze the Model: Distribute a copy of the graphic organizer on page 91 to each student. Guide students through finding the information in the model writing sample to complete the graphic organizer. Some parts of the graphic organizer may not apply.

Write: Assign and provide copies of one or both writing tasks on pages 92 and 93 or let students choose. Also provide copies of the graphic organizer. Make sure students understand the task before beginning. If needed, brainstorm ideas as a class to complete the graphic organizer. Then have students write their news reports.

Extend: If desired, have students brainstorm some additional topics that they want to investigate and write about. Have them complete the extension activity on page 93 on a separate sheet of paper.

Investigative Reporting

Leeza is a reporter for her school newspaper. She writes about events that happen at school and in the neighborhoods around the school. Leeza was asked to investigate reports of odd, loud noises on the school grounds and to write an article for the paper.

Peacocks Come to School

by Leeza Asaad

If your concentration has been broken by loud screams out of nowhere, you've heard from our latest school-family members. A male peacock and its mate, called a peahen, have decided to roost in the pine trees on the south side of the school along Justin Drive.

Peacocks have long, colorful feathers and a loud call used to attract mates or scare off predators. It can be heard miles away. Some of our teachers say their call sounds like the screams of a child being hurt. No one describes them as musical!

Peacocks actually make a wide variety of sounds: screams, honks, squawks, moans, and even a donkey sound. They all mean something different.

Mrs. Harris, who lives on Justin Drive, jumps every time they call. She tried to scare them away, but they kept returning. Mr. Sarabia, who teaches 2nd grade, thinks the birds are intelligent. His class observes the birds every day.

Name ____________________

News Report Graphic Organizer

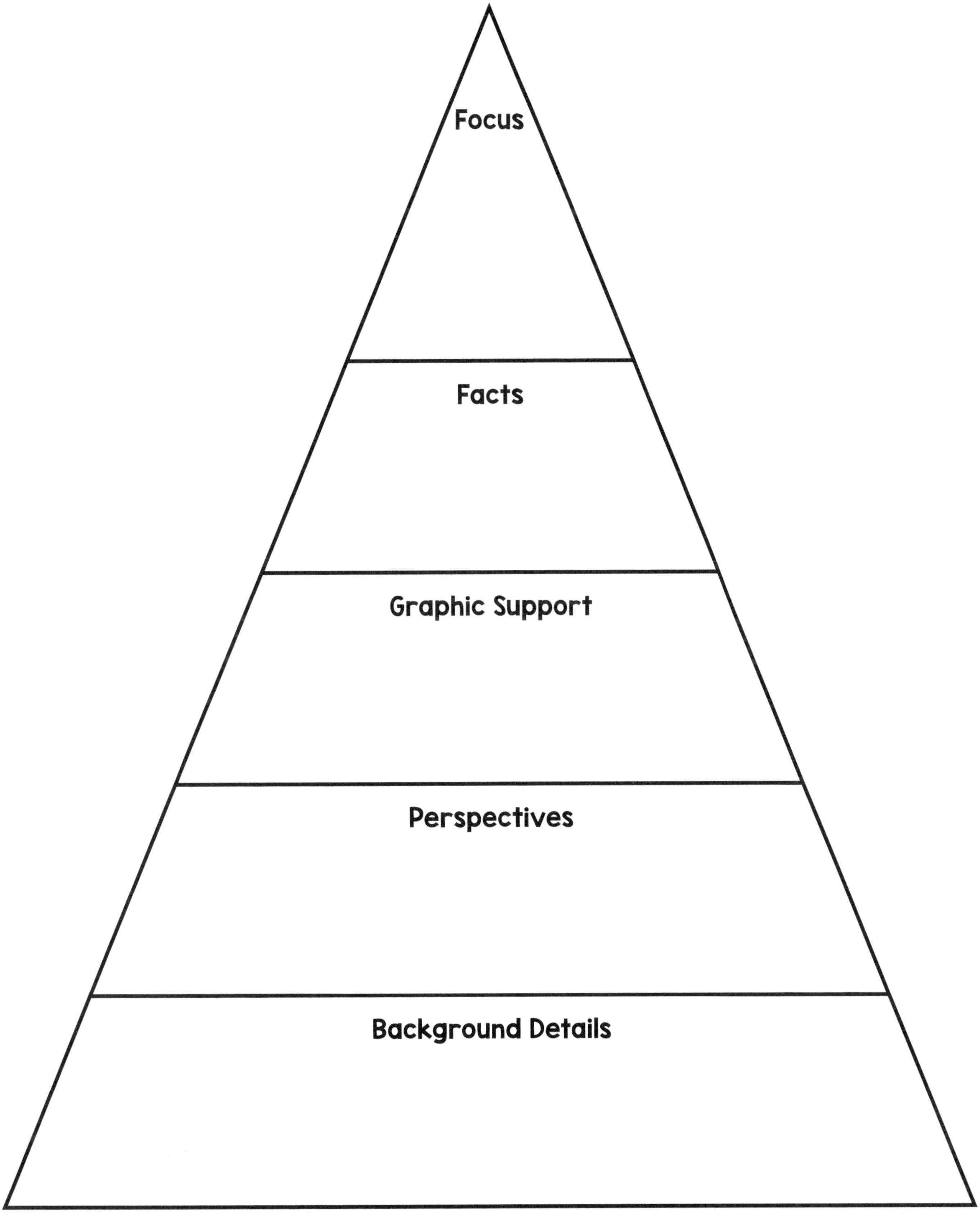

Name ____________________

Weather Report Writing Task #1

Imagine that you are a meteorologist for a TV news channel in Australia. You are going to give a forecast for tomorrow's weather. Research Australia's weather. Then write what you will say about the temperature, rain, wind, or other weather conditions. Draw weather icons on the map.

Name ______________________

World Report Writing Task #2

Imagine that you are a foreign correspondent, covering news in other countries. Choose an interesting event that may affect your country and write a report on it. Explain who caused the event and write details of what happened and where it took place. Then explain why the event may affect other places.

Extension Activity

Think of an issue, a person, or a topic that interests you. Write a report on it for a magazine that covers similar information.

Be Brief

A summary gives a short description of what something or someone says or does. You can summarize a book, an article, a blog, a movie, or any other media. You can summarize what your teacher said during a lesson or what someone said in a speech. You can summarize what happened in gym class when Susie found a spider in her shoe!

Any story or topic can be summarized for another person or even for yourself. A summary helps you remember information later without having to re-read or re-watch all the way through again. It can give others an idea of what something is about so they can decide if they want to read or watch the whole thing. A summary simplifies an idea or a story; it should not recap every action or contain any dialogue.

A summary should contain the following:

- the title or source, as appropriate
- the author's main points and main supporting ideas
- the author's interpretations and conclusions of nonfiction concepts
- a basic description of the people and main events of a narrative
- the writer's own words, using language appropriate for the audience
- only information from the original source, not the writer's interpretation

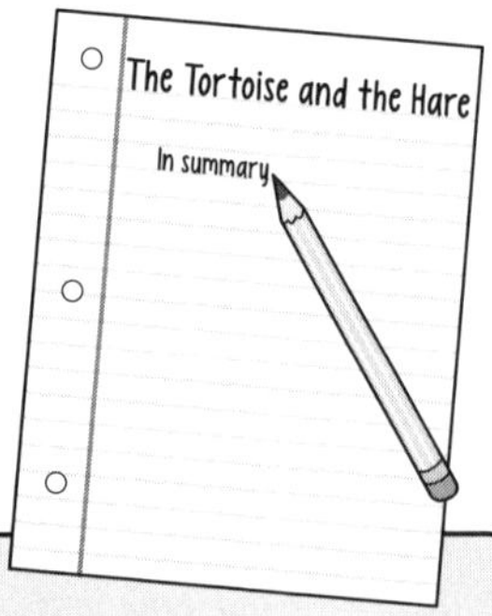

The Lesson

Introduce: Using the information above, explain to students what a summary is. Then distribute a copy of page 95 to each student and have them read the scenario. Discuss it, asking students if they have ever summarized anything for someone else and why they did it.

Look at a Model: Have students read the model writing sample, "Fable Summary." Discuss it, asking students if they are familiar with the fable. Do they think Penny will want Xander to read the whole fable to her now? Ask whether they think anything could be added or changed in the summary.

Analyze the Model: Distribute a copy of the graphic organizer on page 96 to each student. Guide students through finding the information in the model writing sample to complete the graphic organizer. Some parts of the graphic organizer may not apply.

Write: Assign and provide copies of one or both writing tasks on pages 97 and 98 or let students choose. Also provide copies of the graphic organizer. Make sure students understand the task before beginning. If needed, brainstorm ideas as a class to complete the graphic organizer. Then have students write their summaries.

Extend: If desired, have students brainstorm situations in their own lives in which they might need to write a summary. Have them complete the extension activity on page 98 on a separate sheet of paper.

Story Time

Xander was going to read the story *The Tortoise and the Hare* to Penny, his younger sister. Penny thinks surprises are scary, so she asked him what it was about before he started reading. Here is Xander's summary.

Fable Summary

The Tortoise and the Hare is a type of story called a fable. The author's name is Aesop. This fable is about a hare who likes to show off. He's always making fun of the slow tortoise, who challenges the hare to a race. During the race, the hare gets way ahead but decides to take a nap before reaching the end. The tortoise passes the hare. The hare wakes up just before the tortoise crosses the finish line. The tortoise wins. The point of the story is that if you just keep going, even slowly, you will always finish, maybe even first.

Name ____________________

Summary Graphic Organizer

Topic, Story, or Source

1st Point or Event

2nd Point or Event

3rd Point or Event

4th Point or Outcome

Name ______________________

Article Summary Writing Task #1

Adam wrote the following article for his school newspaper. Write a summary of Adam's article.

Ramps

Most places—such as grocery stores, restaurants, office buildings, buses, and hotels—haven't always had wheelchair ramps. In many parts of the world, they still don't require these ramps. I use a wheelchair. I can't imagine how hard it would be to get around without them.

I dream about what I want to be someday. I want to have the same career choices as other kids. I don't want to be limited to jobs only in places with wheelchair ramps.

Some people think wheelchair ramps are too expensive for so few people. But these ramps can help everyone. They help truckers move goods into a store. Shoppers use them for their carts. Parents push baby strollers up and down ramps. Travelers need ramps to move their wheeled luggage.

Ramps benefit just about everyone. They are worth the money to install them. There should be laws everywhere requiring ramps.

Name ____________________

Story Summary Writing Task #2

Imagine that the Drama Club is going to act out a childhood story for the youngest students in your school. Write a summary of a childhood story that you think they should choose, such as *Goldilocks and the Three Bears, The Little Prince, Cinderella,* or any other story you think they would enjoy.

Extension Activity

Think of something interesting or dramatic that happened at school or in your neighborhood recently. Summarize what happened for your friends or family.

Decisions, Decisions

Decisions can be difficult when no choice is perfect. Each option often has both positive aspects and negative aspects. For example, if you try out for the school play, you'll have to give up jogging three afternoons each week. But the chosen play is one of your favorites, and you might not have another opportunity to perform it.

When you're having trouble deciding something, making a pro–con list can help. Sometimes writing all the arguments for and against lets you consider all the angles and decide which is most important to you. There may be more factors on one side than the other, which might indicate what to do. However, you might ultimately choose the side with fewer factors if they are more compelling. Often, just the exercise of listing pros and cons triggers hidden feelings that lead you to a choice.

A pro–con list should contain the following:

- a statement about what is being decided
- two columns—one labeled *pro* (for) and one labeled *con* (against)
- reasons in each column

Alternatively, the list could also be used to show the benefits of two choices, such as choosing to wear sandals or boots today, with one column for each.

The Lesson

Introduce: Using the information above, explain to students what a pro–con list is. Then distribute a copy of page 100 to each student and have them read the scenario. Discuss it, asking students how they make similar decisions. Ask if they have ever written a pro–con list.

Look at a Model: Have students read the model writing sample, "Money Decision." Discuss it, asking what factors Li Wei included on his pro–con list. Ask what decision your students might make based on this list. Ask whether they think anything could be added or changed on the list.

Analyze the Model: Distribute a copy of the graphic organizer on page 101 to each student. Guide students through finding the information in the model writing sample to complete the graphic organizer. Some parts of the graphic organizer may not apply.

Write: Assign and provide copies of one or both writing tasks on pages 102 and 103 or let students choose. Also provide copies of the graphic organizer. Make sure students understand the task before beginning. If needed, brainstorm ideas as a class to complete the graphic organizer. Then have students write their lists.

Extend: If desired, have students brainstorm online situations in their own lives in which they would need to write a pro–con list. Have them complete the extension activity on page 103 on a separate sheet of paper.

Happy New Year!

During the New Year holiday, Li Wei received some money from his grandparents. He's trying to decide if he wants to use it to buy something sweet or save it. He wrote the following pro–con list to help him decide.

Money Decision

SHOULD I BUY SOMETHING SWEET WITH MY NEW YEAR'S MONEY?

PRO	CON
I like sweets—they make me happy.	Sweets aren't healthy for my body or my teeth.
The cashier at the store is nice. She says business is slow. I'd like to support her business.	If I save my money, maybe I could buy something even better later.
I would have fun taking a trip to the store with my grandparents.	My parents are always telling me that it's important to save money.
My grandparents would like to see me enjoy the money they gave me. If I save it, they wouldn't get to do that.	Once I eat a sweet, it's gone forever. Maybe a toy, or something else that lasts, would be better.

Name ______________________________

Pro-Con List Graphic Organizer

What am I deciding between?

Things I could benefit from:

Things I would give up:

How others would be affected:

Name ______________________________

Getting a Pet Writing Task #1

Imagine that your family is discussing getting a pet. Choose a pet that you might like. Then research what is involved with having that pet, such as the cost and the kind of care it needs. Find out how long it lives and what kind of food it eats. Ask people who have had this pet what they think about it. Then write a pro–con list for getting this pet.

DECISION: ______________________________

PRO	CON

Name ____________________

Using Spare Time Writing Task #2

Imagine that you are nearly always busy with school, sports practice, and babysitting your younger siblings. At the end of the month, your siblings will be away at science camp, and you will be in between basketball and track season. A friend is trying to find volunteers to help out with a Special Olympics event. You'd love to help, but you were looking forward to some time to relax. Write a pro–con list to help you decide whether you should volunteer.

DECISION: ____________________

PRO	CON

Extension Activity

Think of an upcoming decision in your life. It can be for something coming soon, such as what to do this weekend. Or it can be for something in the future, such as choosing a career or a place you might like to live. Write a pro–con list.

Look More Closely | **Lab Report**

Eureka!

Doing science experiments is exciting. Experiments let you experience how science works. Science helps us solve problems and develop new technology. It keeps us healthy, helps us solve crimes, and expands access to our world and to worlds beyond. Most working scientists are involved in applying known principles to new situations, but they might make a new discovery to present to the world.

Much of science involves observation, brainstorming, and researching, along with testing out hypotheses in formal experiments. Scientists have a standard format for conducting and documenting experiments. The standard format of a lab report includes the question being explored, a hypothesis, existing research on the topic, and a list of materials and procedures used, along with the results.

The results on a lab report should contain the following:

- the question and hypothesis of the experiment
- data and observations from the experiment
- analysis of the data and observations
- a conclusion that addresses the hypothesis
- facts and science-based interpretation; no opinions
- formal style with correct spelling, grammar, and punctuation

The Lesson

Introduce: Using the information above, explain to students what a lab report is and how the components relate to each other. Then distribute page 105 to students and have them read the scenario. Discuss it, asking students about their experiences doing science experiments.

Look at a Model: Have students read the model writing sample, "Experiment Results." Discuss it, asking students if they understood the science experiment and what was discovered. Ask whether they think anything could be added or changed in the results.

Analyze the Model: Distribute a copy of the graphic organizer on page 106 to each student. Guide students through finding the information in the model writing sample to complete the graphic organizer. Some parts of the graphic organizer may not apply.

Write: Assign and provide copies of one or both writing tasks on pages 107 and 108 or let students choose. Also provide copies of the graphic organizer. Make sure students understand the task before beginning. If needed, brainstorm ideas as a class to complete the graphic organizer. Then have students write their science results.

Extend: If desired, have students brainstorm science events that they wonder about or are interested in. Have them complete the extension activity on page 108 on a separate sheet of paper.

Investigating Bean Growth

Yesika did a science experiment to find out if bean seedlings grow faster under blue light than other colors. She planted 30 seeds under three different colors of light. She measured the plants' heights every week for three weeks. She recorded her data in a table.

Average Height of Bean Seedlings

Time	Blue light	Red light	Green light
after 1 week	0.5 cm	0.5 cm	0.5 cm
after 2 weeks	1.5 cm	1.0 cm	0.75 cm
after 3 weeks	3.0 cm	2.0 cm	1.0 cm

Yesika summarized and analyzed the data and wrote a conclusion. Here is what she wrote.

Experiment Results

All of the plants were the same height when the experiment started. They were still the same height after the first week. But after the second week, differences started to show up. The plant grown in blue light was the tallest, followed by the plant grown in red light. By the end of the third week, the differences were even greater, with the light colors in the same order. My conclusion is that the seedlings grew fastest under the blue light.

Name ______________________________

Science Results Graphic Organizer

Question or hypothesis

Describe any patterns in the data.

Analyze the data patterns: Do they answer or support the question or hypothesis?

If so, what can you conclude?

If not, what can you try next to investigate your question or hypothesis?

Name ______________________________

Paper Airplanes Writing Task #1

Diego did a science fair project in which he tested which paper airplane style flies the farthest. He collected the data below showing how far each plane flew when he threw it. Look at the data and summarize the results. Then write a conclusion about the three styles.

Distance Flown by Different Styles of Paper Airplanes

Trial number	Style #1	Style #2	Style #3
1	10 feet	5 feet	10 feet
2	12 feet	12 feet	15 feet
3	11 feet	4 feet	11 feet
Average	**11 feet**	**7 feet**	**12 feet**

Name ____________________

Musical Mouse Maze Writing Task #2

Parvati did a science experiment to find out if music helps a mouse complete a maze more quickly than silence. She had a mouse run through the same maze 6 times, 3 times with music playing and 3 times without. Look at her data from the maze runs. Then summarize the results and write a conclusion about the effect of music on completing a maze.

Time It Took Mouse to Complete Maze

Trial number	Music?	Time (seconds)
1	yes	82
2	no	94
3	yes	73
4	no	95
5	yes	61
6	no	81

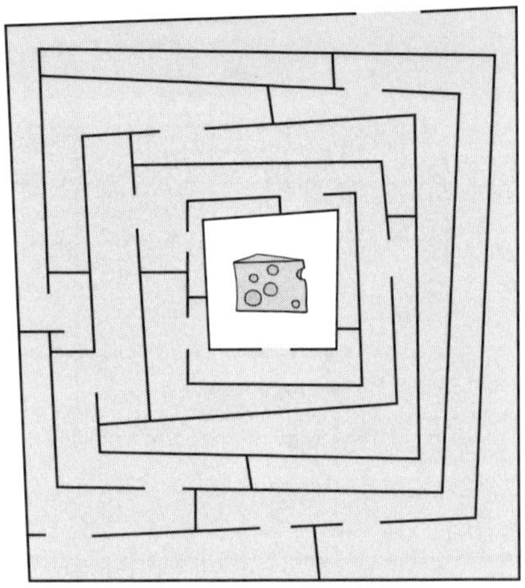

Extension Activity

Think of a science question that you would like to answer. Do some research about it or conduct an experiment to try to answer it. Then write up your science results.

The Big Picture

Billboards are a great way to get people's attention. They can help keep a service or a product, an event or an activity, or a public service message fresh in everyone's mind. They can create a positive impression about their subject. While billboards are usually thought of as advertising, any organization can use a billboard to make the public aware of important issues or to gather support for a good cause.

Many billboards appear on major roadways, but they may also be placed on the sides of buildings and buses. If a message is meant for a specific audience, such as children or truck drivers, the billboard should be placed where that group is most likely to see it. Since many people see billboards for only a few seconds from a distance as they drive by them, the messages should be very short and to the point. Everything should be easy to understand at a glance.

A billboard should contain the following:

- very few words
- a single clear message
- a memorable slogan or funny statement
- a graphic that is easy to understand at a glance
- short directions to a nearby location, if applicable

The Lesson

Introduce: Using the information above, explain to students what a billboard is. Then distribute page 110 and have students read the scenario. Discuss it, asking students if they can remember billboards that they have seen and what made them memorable. Ask what they liked about the billboards.

Look at a Model: Have students read the model writing sample, "Bus Stop Billboard." Discuss it, asking students how they would react if they saw this billboard every day. Ask whether they think anything could be added or changed to make the billboard more effective.

Analyze the Model: Distribute a copy of the graphic organizer on page 111 to each student. Guide students through finding the information in the model writing sample to complete the graphic organizer. Some parts of the graphic organizer may not apply.

Write: Assign and provide copies of one or both writing tasks on pages 112 and 113 or let students choose. Also provide copies of the graphic organizer. Make sure students understand the task before beginning. If needed, brainstorm ideas as a class to complete the graphic organizer. Then have students design and write their billboards.

Extend: If desired, have students brainstorm how people in different jobs might use billboards. Have them complete the extension activity on page 113 on a separate sheet of paper.

Dentist Ad

Olivia Juarez's mom is a dentist. She plans to put a billboard at all the school bus stops to remind kids to brush their teeth daily. Since it is aimed at kids, she asked her daughter to design the billboard, hoping that Olivia would know best how to communicate with other kids. Here is Olivia's billboard design.

Bus Stop Billboard

Name ____________________________

Billboard Graphic Organizer

Text ideas

Purpose of billboard

Problem to solve

Possible billboard locations

Picture ideas

Name ______________________________

Anti-Bullying Writing Task #1

Bullying in school is a terrible problem. Imagine that you work for an organization that helps prevent bullying and assists kids who are bullied in school. Design a billboard that discourages kids from bullying others.

Name ______________________________

Refreshment Writing Task #2

Some of the most common billboards are for food—especially fast food—and sodas. Choose your favorite food or drink. Imagine that you work for a company that sells that item. Design a billboard to advertise it and encourage others to buy it.

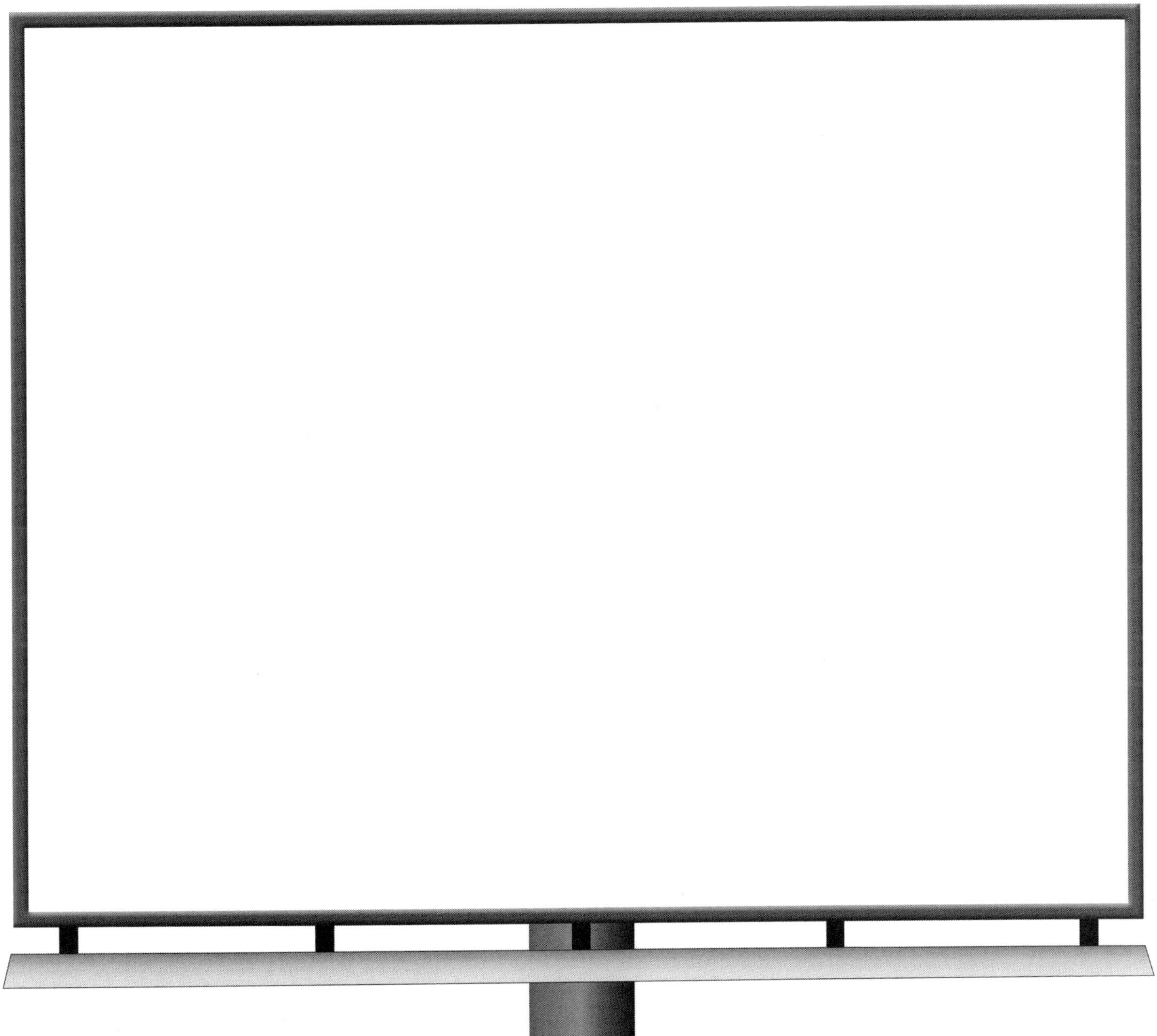

Extension Activity

Think about a career that you would like to have when you grow up. Then design a billboard to help with something in your chosen career. For example, if you plan to be a race car driver, your billboard might remind people about safe driving. If you plan to be an athlete, your billboard could advertise an upcoming game. If you'd like to run for mayor, design a billboard to get votes.

What a Deal!

Catalogs are online or printed lists of items for sale. Many people enjoy looking through catalogs from their favorite stores or brands. Others use catalogs to see what options are available for an item they need to buy. Each item is named and is usually shown in a photo. Once a photo catches the customer's eye, he or she wants to know more about the item.

Most catalogs include **copy**, or published text, that describes each item. The copy tries to persuade a potential customer to follow through and make the purchase. The most effective copy gives the reader positive sensory images. It should help people "taste" the cookie, "see" how good they would look in the shirt, or "feel" their strength using the tennis racket. The copy should provide useful details and explain how the customer's life will improve by buying a particular item.

Catalog copy should contain the following:

- an eye-catching title
- the features and benefits of the item
- color and size options and age range, if applicable
- the price
- language appropriate for the intended audience
- correct spelling, grammar, and punctuation

The Lesson

Introduce: Using the information above, explain to students what catalog copy is. Then distribute page 115 and have students read the scenario. Discuss it, asking students about catalogs they have seen. What items did they want to buy? What did they like about the catalogs?

Look at a Model: Have students read the model writing sample, "Take Your Memories with You." Discuss it, asking students what features or benefits buyers will receive. Ask whether they think anything could be added or changed to make the catalog copy more effective.

Analyze the Model: Distribute a copy of the graphic organizer on page 116 to each student. Guide students through finding the information in the model writing sample to complete the graphic organizer. Some parts of the graphic organizer may not apply.

Write: Assign and provide copies of one or both writing tasks on pages 117 and 118 or let students choose. Also provide copies of the graphic organizer. Make sure students understand the task before beginning. If needed, brainstorm ideas as a class to complete the graphic organizer. Then have students write their catalog copy.

Extend: If desired, have students brainstorm activities for which they could write catalog copy. Have them complete the extension activity on page 118 on a separate sheet of paper.

Advertising the Yearbook

The school year is almost over! King Elementary School sells items for graduating students to buy to remember their time there. The items raise money for the school. The upcoming school newsletter has a catalog page advertising these items. Brenda O'Hare is on the school yearbook committee. Brenda wrote the catalog copy for the school yearbook to persuade students to order it.

Take Your Memories with You

As you move on to a new school next year, you won't want to forget your friends and fun times at King Elementary. Buy a yearbook to keep those memories alive! You'll get over 150 pages of classmates' and teachers' photos labeled with their names, as well as photos of all clubs. You can remember the fall carnival, Silly Sports Day, and the spring musical! There are 6 bonus pages in the back for all your friends to sign. Who knows—if one of us becomes famous, your yearbook might be even more valuable! Click here by **May 1** to reserve your yearbook.

Choose from these options:

- ☐ Hardback Yearbook $20
- ☐ Paperback Yearbook $15

Name ______________________________

Catalog Copy Graphic Organizer

Features

Benefits

Catalog copy

for ______________________________

Price and options

Name ____________________

Song Toy Writing Task #1

Imagine that you are writing catalog copy for a new toy for 3-year-old children that teaches them popular children's songs. It lights up, plays music, and glows in the dark. Write catalog copy for this toy. Also draw a picture of the toy. Since most 3-year-olds can't read, the audience for the catalog copy will be parents, grandparents, teachers, or other caregivers for young children.

Name ______________________________

Clothing Catalog Writing Task #2

Imagine that you write for a clothing catalog. Think of your favorite piece of clothing. Write catalog copy for it. Remember to think about its features, such as pockets, the feel of the fabric, or how warm or cool it keeps you. Why would someone like it? Try to communicate how it will make the buyer feel when this item is worn.

Extension Activity

Think about organizations and activities available in your community, such as art and dance classes, sports and fitness activities, or robotics and science clubs. Write catalog copy for a community center catalog to encourage people to join a group that you are familiar with.

Working for Social Justice

Social justice focuses on disadvantages that cause some people to experience challenging situations. These may include being homeless, being an immigrant, living with foster parents, or living in poverty. People in these situations often face additional challenges from these circumstances: hunger, unhealthy conditions, prejudice, lack of safety, unfair treatment, and lack of opportunity.

While charities work to provide quick support for people in need, social justice tries to solve the problems that cause the disadvantages. These problems include a lack of affordable housing, unfair policies, financial troubles, or even environmental problems. There are many nonprofit and humanitarian organizations that can help. These organizations have websites to inform people about the work they do.

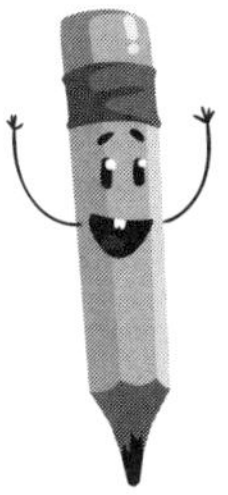

A web page on a website should contain the following:

- good organization that is easy to navigate
- attractive design that is easy to read
- accurate, precise, and relevant information
- persuasive language that uses reasoning and emotions
- graphics that support the text

The Lesson

Introduce: Using the information above, explain to students what a web page is. Then distribute a copy of page 120 to each student and have them read the scenario. Discuss it, asking students what kinds of information they often find on the home page of their favorite websites.

Look at a Model: Have students read the model writing sample, "Sourcefair." Discuss it, asking students what they can figure out about the Sourcefair organization: what problems it works on and how. Ask whether they think anything could be added or changed to better show the organization's purpose.

Analyze the Model: Distribute a copy of the graphic organizer on page 121 to each student. Guide students through finding the information in the model writing sample to complete the graphic organizer. Some parts of the graphic organizer may not apply.

Write: Assign and provide copies of one or both writing tasks on pages 122 and 123 or let students choose. Also provide copies of the graphic organizer. Make sure students understand the task before beginning. If needed, brainstorm ideas as a class to complete the graphic organizer. Then have students do some research and write and design their web pages.

Extend: If desired, have students brainstorm some additional social justice topics that inspire them. Have them complete the extension activity on page 123 on a separate sheet of paper.

The Fairest Flavor of Them All

LaVonne loves chocolate! She even tried to raise a cacao plant to grow her own beans. But these plants grow only near the equator, where the climate is just right. Local workers harvest the beans from cacao pods and send the beans to other places to be made into chocolate. It's a lot of work!

LaVonne learned that farmers who harvest the pods and prepare the beans often don't make enough money to live on. But organizations that encourage fair trade are working to change that. **Fair trade** means paying what something is worth, not just what you can get away with paying. LaVonne volunteers for a fair trade organization called Sourcefair, which asked her to create a home page for its website.

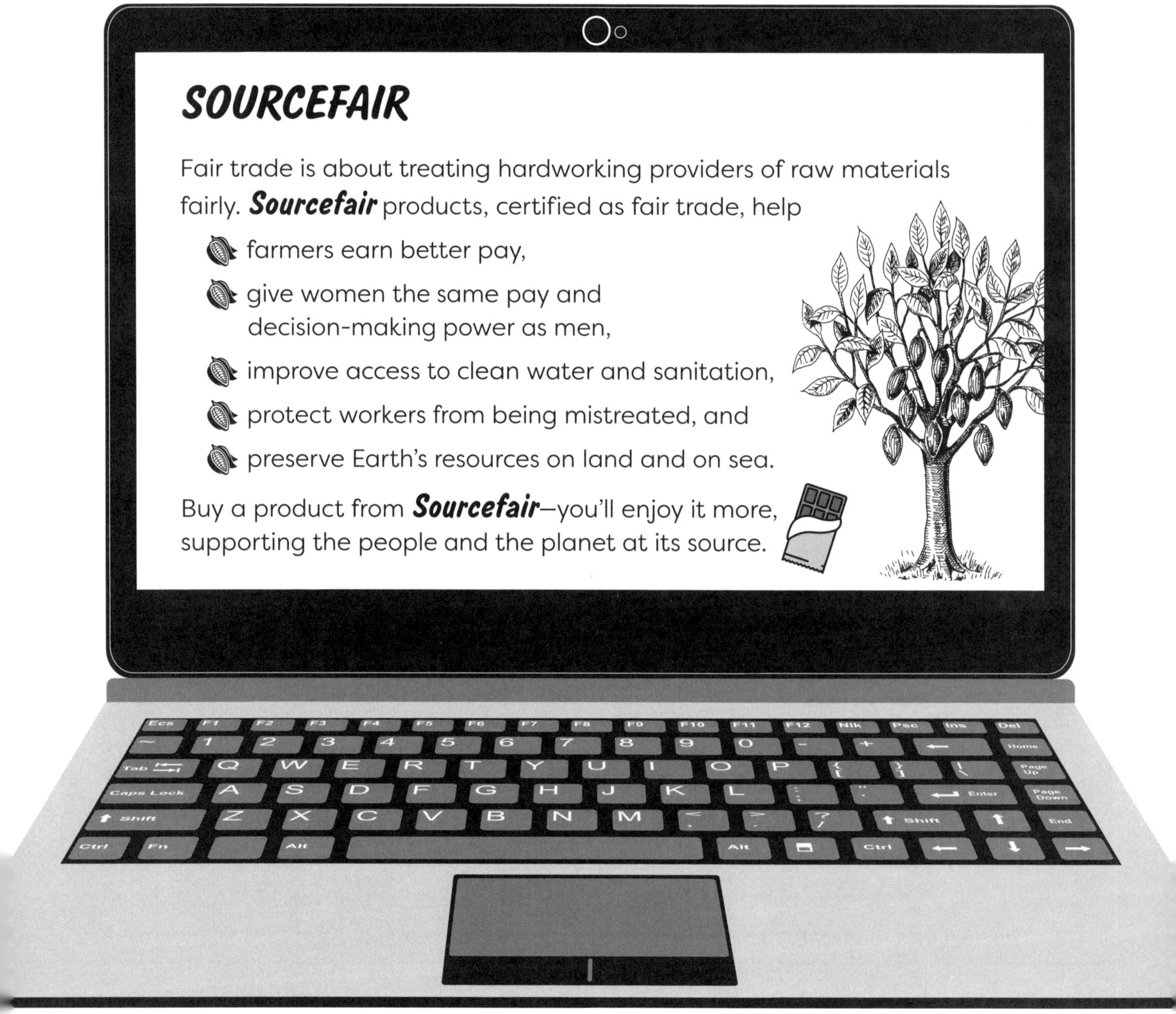

Name ______________________________

Web Page Graphic Organizer

Purpose of web page:

____

____

Important information to include:

____

____

____

Use of persuasive language:

____

____

Organization of information (paragraphs, bullets, diagram, chart, etc.)

____

____

Use of colors, type fonts, and graphics:

____

____

Name ____________________

Community Health Web Page Writing Task #1

Diego lives in a rural community. Ten people who live near a large farm there have been diagnosed with a type of cancer called leukemia in the last year. Diego started a website to track information about the number of people who are sick and the use of chemicals on the farm. Research, write, and design a page for the website that describes the problem and shows supporting statistics. The page should inspire readers to care about and act on the problem.

Name ______________________________

Diversity Club Web Page Writing Task #2

Imagine that your school has a Diversity Club. This club offers activities that different groups of students like. It also tries to resolve conflicts and help different groups understand each other. Write and design a page for the club's website that persuades students to join the club and volunteer their time.

Extension Activity

Choose a social justice issue that you feel strongly about. Find an organization that works on that issue, or imagine what such an organization would do. Write and design a page for its website that persuades people to attend awareness or fundraising events for the organization.

Vote for Me!

From country and city governments to businesses to hobby clubs, almost all organizations have leaders who guide them. Many leaders are elected to their positions by members voting for them. Usually, several candidates run for a position. Often, the voting members do not know the candidates personally. Even if they do, they may need help deciding whom to vote for.

Giving a campaign speech is an important way for someone who is running for an elected office to get the attention and support of potential voters. Candidates need to convince listeners that they will make their lives better—whether in a big or small way—to get as many votes as possible.

A campaign speech should contain the following:

- a short welcome
- brief information about who you are and your qualifications
- the main issues that are important to you and the group
- general ideas for tackling those issues
- conversational language that will appeal to your audience

The Lesson

Introduce: Using the information above, explain to students what a campaign speech is. Then distribute page 125 and have students read the scenario. Discuss it, asking students if they have ever voted for anyone before. Ask how they made their decision, especially if they didn't know the people they were choosing between. Ask if they've ever heard a campaign speech and what they liked and didn't like about it.

Look at a Model: Have students read the model writing sample, "Citlali Cruz for President." Discuss it, asking students what they think of Citlali as a candidate. Ask whether they think anything could be added or changed to make the speech more effective.

Analyze the Model: Distribute a copy of the graphic organizer on page 126 to each student. Guide students through finding the information in the model writing sample to complete the graphic organizer. Some parts of the graphic organizer may not apply.

Write: Assign and provide copies of one or both writing tasks on pages 127 and 128 or let students choose. Also provide copies of the graphic organizer. Make sure students understand the task before beginning. If needed, brainstorm ideas as a class to complete the graphic organizer. Then have students write their campaign speeches.

Extend: If desired, have students brainstorm situations in their own lives in which they might need to write a campaign speech. Have them complete the extension activity on page 128 on a separate sheet of paper.

A New Leader

Citlali's favorite subject is Spanish, and she joined the Spanish Club the first week of school. While she enjoys its activities, she doesn't think the club is doing enough. She is running for president of the Spanish Club so she can change that. She wrote the following speech.

Citlali Cruz for President

Hola and bienvenidos, members of the Spanish Club!

As a member for the past year, I'd appreciate your vote for me as president of the club. I love this club! In addition to speaking Spanish, we sometimes do cultural activities from Spanish-speaking countries around the world. For example, last year, our club ate at a Mexican restaurant and saw a play written by a Puerto Rican playwright. But we could do much more.

My first name means "star." As your star president, I'd like to shine a light on more cultures and expand our activities. For example, we could go to a Cuban music concert, hold a Salvadoran *pupusa* cook-off competition, arrange an Argentine tango class, and visit a Peruvian art exhibit. This would make our club more fun for current members. Plus, if we let nonmembers participate, we could maybe get them to join. These activities will educate students and even teachers about the importance of Spanish-speaking cultures and the Spanish language. I'll ask the student council for more money. We can also hold some of these events as fundraisers.

I know that all of you appreciate the contributions of Spanish cultures. I hope you agree that we should shine more light on these contributions and that you'll elect me to make it happen. Thank you for listening, and please remember to vote for Citlali Cruz!

Name ______________________________

Campaign Speech Graphic Organizer

____,
(name)

candidate for ______________________________________
(position)

☐ Welcome

☐ Who I am, my qualifications

☐ Why I'm running

☐ Issues facing voters

☐ Solutions to issues

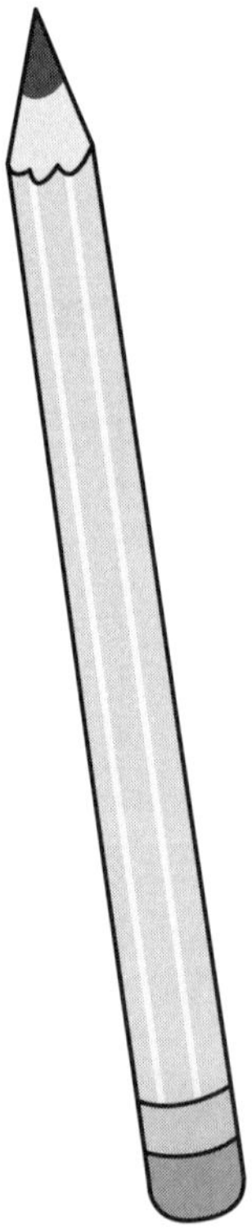

Name ______________________________

Neighborhood Board Writing Task #1

Many apartment buildings, condo complexes, and other neighborhood associations have boards that handle repairs and services that affect everyone who lives there. They also make rules and resolve conflicts. These boards have elected officers. Imagine that you live in a place with a neighborhood board. Choose one of the positions listed to run for. Write a campaign speech to give to all the people in the neighborhood association.

Positions

President: leads meetings

Treasurer: keeps track of the group's finances

Recording secretary: takes meeting notes

Corresponding secretary: sends out letters and e-mails

Name ____________________

Highest Office Writing Task #2

Imagine that you are running for leader of a country! You choose the country. You have stopped in a small town in that country and need to give a speech to encourage the local people to vote for you. Write a campaign speech about one issue that would be the most important to them. Suggestions include improving schools, having access to clean water and air, making highways and bridges safer, creating jobs, and saving local endangered species.

Extension Activity

Choose a position that you could run for. It could be a position on the student council, a school club or team, or a community organization. Write a campaign speech and deliver it to an audience.